SERIES EDITOR: LEE JOH

OSPREY MILITARY MEN-AT-ARMS 309

THE ITALIAN INVASION OF ABYSSINIA 1935-36

TEXT BY
DAVID NICOLLE

COLOUR PLATES BY
RAFFAELE RUGGERI

OSPREY
MILITARY

First published in Great Britain in 1997 by OSPREY, a division of Reed Books, Michelin House, 81 Fulham Road, London SW3 6RB. Auckland and Melbourne

ISBN 1 85532 692 2

Filmset in Singapore by Pica Ltd.
Printed through World Print Ltd., Hong Kong

Military Editor: Sharon van der Merwe
Design: Alan Hamp @ Design for Books

For a catalogue of all books published by Osprey Military please write to:
Osprey Marketing, Reed Books, Michelin House, 81 Fulham Road, London SW3 6RB

Publisher's Note

Readers may wish to study this title in conjunction with the following Osprey publications:
MAA 282 *Axis Forces in Yugoslavia 1941-45*
MAA169 *Resistance Warfare 1940-45*

Artist's note

THE ITALIAN INVASION OF ABYSSINIA 1935-36

INTRODUCTION

Fitaurari Wasene, the governor of Maji province in the deep south-west of the Ethiopian Empire, photographed in 1926. His official costume, including a long cape and a lion's mane headdress, remained unchanged until the Italian invasion. The Fitaurari's personal guard, with his simple khaki uniform, modern rifle and traditional leather shield, was also typical of Ethiopian provincial forces. A boy servant or slave carries the Fitaurari's ceremonial fly-whisk, which served as a symbol of rank, and his broad-brimmed sun-hat. (A.W. Hodson photograph, Royal Geographical Society, London)

ETHIOPIA, or Abyssinia as it was known until modern times, is regarded as the oldest Christian country in Africa. It also has a substantial Muslim minority population in the north, the coastal areas and eastern lowlands, as well as tribal peoples who retain animist beliefs. Christianity has been linked to Ethiopia's sense of national identity for centuries, and was also associated with the dominant Tigrean and Amharic highland peoples. The city of Harar in the east of the country remained largely separate from the Christian kingdom of Abyssinia, however, and became a major centre of Islamic civilisation in East Africa,

When Eritrea regained independence in 1993, the Italo-Ethiopian War of 1935-36 began to be seen in a new light. This Red Sea coastal region of ancient Abyssinia was only integrated into the Ethiopian Empire in 1962, and since at least the 7th century AD, when Islam arrived on the offshore islands, its culture was very different from Ethiopia itself. Today, the population of Eritrea consists of roughly equal proportions of Muslims and Christians, although the name Eritrea only dates from 1890 when the Italians derived it from the ancient Latin name for the Red Sea – *Mare Erythraeum*. Islam was the unifying factor among the coastal towns and tribes, just as Christianity was in the highlands. As Islam spread, so the centre of gravity of Christian Ethiopia moved southwards from Axum to Lalibela and Gondar, and finally to Addis Ababa. The Ottoman Turks gradually took control of the coastal ports, eventually passing control to the Egyptians in the 19th century. Somalia never formed part of the Ethiopian kingdom. The interior was inhabited by Somali nomads, while the coastal ports were dominated by Arab merchant communities who fluctuated between independence and nominal recognition of the suzerainty of the main Muslim power in the western Indian Ocean.

A private Italian trading company purchased Assab in southern Eritrea in 1869, although since 1840 the British had an outpost on the northern Somali coast. Meanwhile Egypt, which already occupied the Sudan, extended its authority down

3

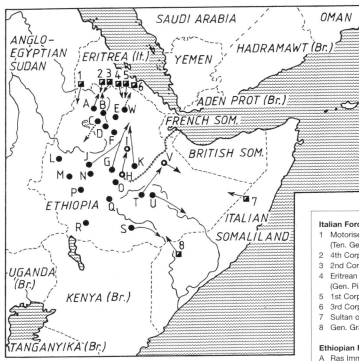

Italian Forces
1. Motorised Column (Ten. Gen. Starace).
2. 4th Corps (Gen. Babbini).
3. 2nd Corps (Gen. Maravigna).
4. Eritrean Corps (Gen. Pirzio-Biroli).
5. 1st Corps (Gen. Santini).
6. 3rd Corps (Gen. Baftico)
7. Sultan of Olol Dinle.
8. Gen. Graziani.

Ethiopian Forces
A. Ras Immiru.
B. Degiacc Admassu Burru.
C. Gessesse Beiew (Army of Gojjam; deserts).
D. Haile Kebbede (Army of Wag).
E. Ras Seyum (Army of Tigre).
F. Ras Cassa (Army of Beghemder).
G. Ras Mulughieta (*Mahel Safari* 'Army of the Centre').
H. Emperor Haile Selassie (*Kebur Zabagna* 'Imperial Guard', at Addis Ababa).
I. Crown Prince (Army of Wollo, at Dese).
J. Bitwoded Makonnen (Army of Wollega).
K. Ras Kebbede & Degiacc Aberra Tedia (Army of Shoa).
L. Ras Mangasha Wube.
M. Degiacc Makonnen Endalkatchew (Army of Illub Abor).
N. Degiacc Hapta Mariam.
O. Degiacc Mangasha Wolde.
P. Ras Getachew Abate.
Q. Degiacc Makonnen Wossene.
R. Degiacc Abebe Damtew (Army of Gemu Gofa).
S. Degiacc Desta Damtew (Army of Sidamo-Borana).
T. Degiacc Amde Mikael (Army of Arusi).
U. Degiacc Biene Merid (Army of Bale).
V. Degiacc Nasibu Zemanuel (Army of Hararge).
W. Degiasmacc Haile Selassie Gugsa (deserts to Italians).

the Red Sea into the Gulf of Aden and around Raas Caseyr (Cape Gardafui) until Ethiopia was virtually surrounded. Then came the Mahdist revolt and the British occupation of Egypt in 1882. Since Britain had no interest in the interior of the Horn of Africa, London encouraged others to take over from existing Egyptian garrisons. As a result the Italian government bought Assab from

The banner of the *Mahel Safari* or traditional Ethiopian 'Army of the Centre' was given to this force in 1934. It is decorated with an embroidered picture of St George and the Dragon, and was regarded as the War Flag of the Ethiopian army as a whole. It is also worth noting that the soldiers carrying this important banner are wearing traditional Ethiopian costume rather than modern-style uniforms.

An Ethiopian horseman who is almost certainly a member of the aristocracy because of his lionskin headdress and lionskin *lembd* or cape. Apart from the magnificence of his costume, shield and horse-harness, it is interesting to note that the man rides with a very simple, almost primitive, stirrup for the big toe only.

the private trading company and in 1885 sent two military expeditions to the ex-Turco-Egyptian port of Massawa in Eritrea. The Ethiopians moved into the Eritrean highlands and took control of Harar in the east, areas which had been held by Egypt. As the Italians pushed inland from Massawa, and the Ethiopian governor of Tigre probed northwards, there were inevitable clashes before the Treaty of Ucciali (1889) made Ethiopia an Italian 'protectorate'. Further Italian expansion during the anarchy which followed the death of the Ethiopian Emperor John culminated in disaster at the battle of Adwa (Adowa) in 1896, which not only forced Italy to recognise Ethiopian independence, but inflicted huge damage on Italian self-esteem. A less important result of Adwa was the foundation of Addis Ababa as Ethiopia's new capital. Originally consisting of Emperor Menelik's hilltop *gibbi* or palace, it was soon surrounded by the *gibbis* of other *rases*, or noblemen.

Italian progress in Somalia suffered no such setback. In 1885 outposts were established on the Indian Ocean coast by treaty with the Sultan of Zanzibar, titular ruler of the area. Three years later, the local Sultan of Hobyo (Obbia) accepted an Italian protectorate and became Italy's loyal ally. By 1891 the Italian flag flew over the entire coast from Raas Caseyr to the Jubba River. For several years the Italian government leased trading rights and the obligation to maintain order to a private company, but it proved unable to cope with increasing local resistance led by Muhammad Ibn 'Abd Allah Assan, the so-called 'Mad Mullah', who was neither mad nor a mullah, but actually a notable Somali poet and patriot. As a result the Italian state took over direct control of Italian Somaliland in 1905. Meanwhile, the Ethiopians had moved no further east than the city of Harar, leaving the lowlands of the Ogaden Desert to those nomadic Somali tribes who also dominated the interiors of Italian and British Somaliland.

The situation changed dramatically during the First World War, when the Emperor Lij Jasu converted to Islam, made an alliance with Muhammad Ibn 'Abd Allah Assan and offered to put Ethiopia under the spiritual authority of the Ottoman Turkish sultan-caliph. His action has often been described as an act of insanity, but in reality Lij Jasu hoped to harness the warlike Somalis and the Muslim Galla tribes of eastern Ethiopia to crush the rebellious *rases*, or nobles, and unify his country. He also hoped for backing from the Ottoman army stationed in Arabia, and from German forces in Tanganyika. But this gamble failed, and Lij Jasu was toppled by the *rases* led by Ras Tafari Makonnen in September 1916. His ally, the 'Mad Mullah' Muhammad Ibn 'Abd Allah Assan, was attacked by British, French and Italian troops in Somalia. A month later Ras Tafari Makonnen led his private army into Harar and massacred a large part of the Muslim population, including many Somalis. This act left a legacy of bitterness against the dominant Amharic Christian

Ethiopians which would bear fruit in 1935-36.

Despite his victory, at the age of 25 Ras Tafari was considered too young to become *Negus Negast*, or emperor, himself. Instead, Zauditu, daughter of the previous Emperor Menelik, was proclaimed empress while Ras Tafari became 'heir apparent', and regent. They held power in the capital while aristocratic *rases* dominated the provinces. Ras Tafari's own powerbase was Harar, where his father Ras Makonnen had been governor and, like his father, Ras Tafari was a dedicated moderniser.

While ex-Emperor Lij Jasu fled to the Denakil Mountains of southern Eritrea, the 'Mad Mullah' was recognised by the Ottomans as ruler of Somalia in 1917. In fact, Muhammad Ibn 'Abd Allah Assan was not as isolated as might be supposed, for on the other side of the Gulf of Aden the Ottoman Turkish General 'Ali Said Pasha penned a British garrison in Aden and smuggled rifles to the Somalis throughout the First World War. The Sultan of Hobyo's private army and several other coastal Somali tribes remained loyal to the Italians. As a result the Italian army's *Regio Corpo Truppe Coloniali* (Royal Corps of Colonial Troops) developed into a highly effective force by 1917.

The end of the Great War did not bring peace to Ethiopia, where a multi-sided struggle for power continued. The Muslim Lij Jasu was captured by Empress Zauditu in 1921, but the Christian Ras Tafari

LEFT Eritrean warriors, probably Tigrinya, in traditional costume photographed only a few years before the Italian invasion of Ethiopia. These warlike men formed the backbone of the Italian army's colonial forces in East Africa. Their native weapons were virtually identical to those of the neighbouring northern Ethiopians and included a highly decorated shield and a *shotel* curved sabre. (A. Baratti photograph)

BELOW Three soldiers of the Ethiopian *Zabagna* gendarmerie of Addis Ababa photographed in the autumn of 1935. The Imperial Guard was effectively an offshoot of this *Zabagna*, while the *Zabagna* itself, though uniformed in European style, was never as well equipped as the Imperial Guard.

Makonnen continued to implement his ideas of a unified country with a strong central government. Bitter opposition to Ras Tafari's modernisation now came from the aged minister of war, Fitaurari Hapta Giorghis, resulting in civil war in the northern province of Tigre, where the local *rases* seemed incapable of deciding whom to support. Fitaurari Hapta died in 1926, but even this did not bring stability, for now Ras Tafari and Empress Zauditu came to blows. Two years later Ras Tafari Makonnen finally emerged triumphant and Zauditu agreed that he be crowned *Negus Negast* on her death. Even so, the next two years saw Ras Tafari's troops crushing a rebellion by Zauditu's divorced husband, Ras Gugsa Walda, around the old Abyssinian capital of Gondar. This campaign saw the first military use of aircraft in Ethiopia, though the Italians had brought an antique Farman 5B pusher to neighbouring Eritrea to assist in their 'reoccupation' of the colony in 1920.

Finally, on the death of Empress Zauditu in 1930, Ras Tafari Makonnen was crowned emperor and took the name of Haile Selassie. To celebrate this event, France sent a modern Farman aircraft as a gift, while the Italians donated a Breda, both of which joined the tiny Ethiopian Air Force.

Despite having to crush another revolt in Gojjam province in 1932, Emperor Haile Selassie set about modernising his army as fast as

Ethiopia's finances would allow. Since the end of the First World War he had followed a very anti-Italian policy, probably because he feared Italian involvement in the country's civil wars. Foreign advisers were recruited from anywhere except Italy, even after a new Italo-Ethiopian treaty in 1928, and this caused deep frustration in Rome. Swiss, Belgians and Swedes modernised the army, French and Germans doing the same for the air force. Partly as a consequence, the Italian Ministry of Overseas Territories began drawing up plans for an invasion of Ethiopia in 1932, following their crushing of resistance in Italian-ruled Libya. A new commander was also appointed for the Italian army, two years before the Wal Wal incident triggered a chain of events which culminated in war.

CHRONOLOGY

3 November 1934 Ethiopian force arrives at Italian-garrisoned Wal Wal, within Ethiopian territory.

5 December 1934 Fighting at Wal Wal, Ethiopians withdraw.

24 December 1934 Mussolini orders Gen. Emilio De Bono to Eritrea to take command of the proposed invasion army.

27 December 1934 Mussolini orders full mobilisation in Somaliland, and partial mobilisation in Eritrea.

7 January 1935 Italian-French Agreement secures French non-involvement in the Ethiopian crisis.

18 July 1935 Emperor Haile Selassie warns his people of approaching war.

28 September 1935 *Maskal* religious festival in Ethiopia and Eritrea is marked by military parades.

2 October 1935 Mussolini addresses a crowd in Rome; Italian forces move up to the Ethiopian frontier.

3 October 1935 Italian forces enter Ethiopia; Ethiopian Empire declares war on Italy.

Northern Front

4 October 1935 Italians occupy Adigrat, Inticho and Daro Tacle.

6 October 1935 Italians take Adwa.

10 October 1935 Degiasmacc Haile Selassie Gugsa, commander of the Mek'ele sector, defects to Italians.

15 October 1935 Ancient Ethiopian capital of Axum falls to the Italians.

8 November 1935 Mek'ele falls to the Italians.

16 November 1935 Salaclaca falls to Italians.

28 November 1935 Pietro Badoglio replaces De Bono as Italian commander in East Africa.

15 December 1935 Ethiopians, having gathered their forces, counter-attack Italian forces at the Dembeguina Pass; force Gran Sasso Division to withdraw and retake the Scire area.

22 December 1935 First Italian use of poisoned gas.

20 January 1936, Badoglio reopens the Italian offensive at first battle of Tembien between the Warieu Pass and Mek'ele.

22-23 January 1936 Ethiopians encircle Italians at the Warieu Pass and make continuous assaults on Italian positions.

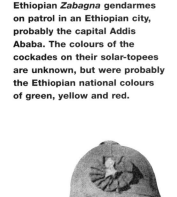

Ethiopian *Zabagna* gendarmes on patrol in an Ethiopian city, probably the capital Addis Ababa. The colours of the cockades on their solar-topees are unknown, but were probably the Ethiopian national colours of green, yellow and red.

24 January 1936 End of the battle of Tembien results in a draw though the Ethiopian offensive is halted.

10-15 February 1936 Battle of Enderta, Italians take Amba Aradam.

27 February-2 March 1936 Second Battle of Tembien, Italians take Worq Amba.

31 March 1936 Battle of Maych'ew, Italians defeat counteroffensive by the main Ethiopian army including the Imperial Guard under Emperor Haile Selassie.

Southern Front

4 October 1935 Italians occupy Dolo Odo and Maladdaie on the Genale (Jubba) River.

6 October 1935 Fortress of Gedlegube falls to Italians; Italians reach K'orahe minefield in the Ogaden Desert.

21 October 1935 Sultan of Olol Dinle (the Somali ally of Italians) occupies Geladi.

30 of October 1935 Italians and Ethiopians clash on the River Dawa.

Lancers of the Kebur Zabagna, or Ethiopian Imperial Guard cavalry, parading outside the Emperor's *gibbi* or palace in 1935. The two officers can be distinguished by the lionskin on the top of their caps. They, and the troopers, also have swords attached to their saddles.

11 November 1935 Italians intercept and defeat a motorised Ethiopian relief column near Hamaniei.

25 November 1935 Fighting at Lama Scillindi.

28 November 1935 Italians bomb Degeh Bur.

29 December 1935 Sultan of Olol Dinle's troops in action against Ethiopians at Golle.

31 December 1935 Italians occupy Denan.

5 January 1936 Fighting at Areri.

12-16 January 1936 Battle of Genale Wenz, Italians defeat southernmost Ethiopian army.

16 January 1936 Large-scale desertions of Christian *askaris* from Eritrean colonial battalions in Somalia, many join Ethiopians.

19 January 1936 Italians reach the wells of Ogobo.

20 January 1936 Italians reach main Ethiopian military base at Negele, take Borana.

14 April 1936 Italians start major thrust towards Harar.

15 April 1936 Italians take Warandab and Gorile.

18 April 1936 Italian army's Libyan Division in battle near Bircot wells.

21 April 1936 Italians take Dovalle.

22 April 1936 Italians take El Fud.

23 April 1936 Italians take Segag; Ethiopians evacuate Daga Medo.

24-25 April 1936 Italian offensive against Ethiopian fortifications east of Harar; major fighting at Bircot & Gunu Gunu; Ethiopian counter-

RIGHT **Italian infantry in action during the invasion of Ethiopia. The scenery suggests somewhere on the northern front. The picture may have been posed and the machine gun crew are clearly being covered by riflemen while directed by an officer.**

RIGHT BELOW **Lt. Gen. Starace with his *Colonna Celere* of *bersaglieri* light infantry. The bunches of cockerel feathers in the soldier's solar-topees are very distinctive and the officer in the centre wears shorts.**

BELOW **Infantrymen of the *Kebur Zabagna* or Ethiopian Imperial Guard exercising with bayonets during a public parade in 1935. These men formed the élite of the Ethiopian army and were almost alone in being equipped and dressed in a completely uniform manner.**

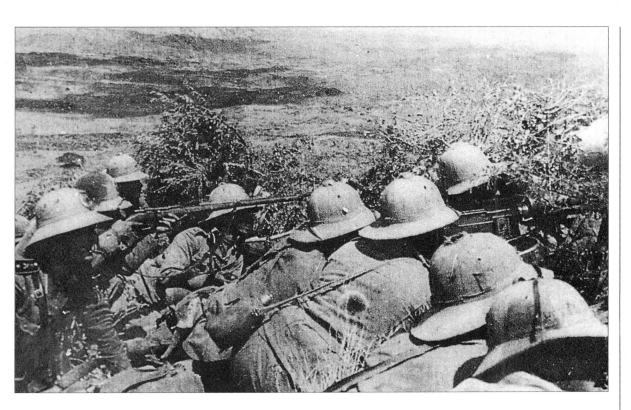

A truckload of Aosta Lancers near Negele, at the southernmost end of the southern front in a region known as the Wadara Forest. The Aosta Lancers were one of the élite units of the Italian army. Originally part of a restructured Piedmontese Army in the 1830s, they played a leading role in the struggle for Italian unification. During the Italian-Ethiopian war they were in the southern column commanded by Graziani.

attack at Daga Medo delays Italian attack on Degeh Bur; Italians take Daga Medo, Bircot, Hamanei.

30 April 1936 Italian forces take Degeh Bur, effectively marking the defeat of the Ethiopian army.

6 May 1936 Italians occupy Jijiga.

8 May 1936 Italians occupy Harar.

9 May 1936 Italians occupy Dire Dawa.

5 May 1936 Italian forces enter the Ethiopian capital, Addis Ababa.

10 May 1936 Italian troops from Northern and Southern Fronts link up at Dire Dawa.

Men of the 221st 'Italiani all'Estero' Legion of the MVSN Fascist Militia, detrucking near the front. This unit of 'Black Shirts', as they were popularly known, consisted of Italian emigrants from foreign countries who volunteered for service during the invasion of Ethiopia. Their training was, however, limited.

THE ETHIOPIAN ARMY

Ras Tafari, or Emperor Haile Selassie as he was now called, came to power at a time when many provincial *rases* had private armies more powerful than his own. It was to counter this challenge that Haile Selassie created a modern army with modern equipment supported by a small air force. Nevertheless, the bulk of Ethiopia's armed forces remained traditional in 1935.

The *chitet*, or muster of the traditional or 'feudal' armies was more medieval than modern. Theoretically, all males from adolescents to old men were supposed to attend, but the numbers who did so reflected the prestige of those calling a *chitet* and their reasons. Ethiopia's pool of military manpower was around one million, as in comparison with its neighbours, the country had a large population. But surviving Ethiopian documents indicate that of these, one-tenth would arrive from loyalty to Christianity, a tenth from loyalty to the Ethiopian Church in particular, a tenth for local loyalties, a tenth only being prepared to serve as guides, a tenth because they needed food or money, a tenth being women, a tenth priests, and so on. Only one-tenth attended out of loyalty to the *Negus Negast*, or emperor, and of these, many were sick or old. Sources anticipated a maximum of 100,000 men to face external invasion; double the number which would fight internal rebellion.

The Ethiopian central government was thought too poor to maintain an army in the field for long, but in the event, Ethiopian soldiers fought for over seven months. A more immediate problem was transporting fighting men from distant parts of the empire to the scene of operations. Regional forces assembled around the *gibbi* of a local *ras* or other leader, while the emperor's own followers assembled in Addis Ababa. Each regional levy had a distinct ethnic content, with Amharan warriors dominating the forces of Gondor, Tigreans those of Tigre. Tigreans were, in fact, regarded as very warlike compared with Amharan peoples and were also traditionally better armed. Haile Selassie's own feudal following came largely from the southern provinces of Harar and Wollo, and was viewed with suspicion by northern forces. Some levies were also more reliable than others; sometimes men from some previously rebellious regions were relegated to guarding herds of cattle. Many Galla nomads attached themselves to the Ethiopian forces as auxiliary cavalry, hoping to harry the enemy's flanks as the main Ethiopian armies included few horsemen. During the Italian-Ethiopian War, however,

Eritrean *askaris* climbing one of the steep mountainsides which dominated warfare on the northern front. Impressed by their élan, the Italians used them as assault troops in several offensives.

NCOs of an Eritrean unit in the *Regio Corpo di Truppe Coloniali* of the Italian army. Three wear the tall *tarbusc* fez of Italian East African colonial recruits, while the fourth has a *bustina* side-cap. The large armbands show their NCO rank.

many Galla went over to the Italians.

Provincial leaders also had their own armed retinues, and membership of these was the highest rank that ordinary Ethiopians could hope for. Men were recruited from unemployed youngsters who hung around the gates of a *gibbi* in the hope of being 'retained' in a *ras*'s service, while the number of such retainers increased a *ras*'s prestige. Many *mekuannent*, or younger aristocrats also joined an army when summoned, usually with servants in tow, while better-off warriors brought wives and children. However, most ordinary warriors had to carry what they needed themselves.

The Ethiopian command structure was very traditional; the emperor was supreme commander during a serious crisis such as foreign invasion. He was supported by the chief officers of state and church who formed a consultative council headed by the *First Fitaurari*, or Minister of War. This was Ras Mulughieta who took over from Birru Wolde Gabriel following the Wal Wal incident of 1934. Beneath them, the command structure was largely provincial, titles such as *Ras, Degiacc, Fitaurari* and *Scium* reflecting local traditions and the status of a leader. Powerful aristocrats who did not govern a specific area but still had armed retinues were similarly given titles reflecting their status. These were honorific rather than specific to a particular military function, despite the fact that some titles had military origins. Nevertheless, such men did form a sort of officer corps.

Titles were very important in Ethiopian society and politics. They were not strictly inherited, though they often passed from father to son, and although the emperor was not the only person permitted to grant titles, his carried more prestige. For example a *fitaurari* created by the emperor was superior to a *fitaurari* created by a *dejaz*. The most senior were the *First Fitaurari* of the Empire (Minister of War), the *Ras be Ras (Ras of Rases)*, and *Ras Bitwoded* (Chancellor). Senior provincial *rases* were entitled to 24 *negarits*, or war-drums, which indicated that they had authority over 24 *degiacc*, or local governors. Yet even the greatest *rases* could not

Ethiopian Titles when used as Military Ranks

Note that the following precise definitions were more theoretical than real.

Ras:	Commander of an army
Degiacc:	Commander of the Threshold
Fitaurari:	Commander of the Advance Guard
Cagnasmacc:	Commander the Right Wing
Grasmacc:	Commander of the Left Wing
Asmacc:	Commander of the Rearguard
Barambaras:	Commander of specialised troops or of a fort
Ietor Abegaz:	Military commander of a district as distinct from the civil governor
Sceleca:	Battalion commander or senior soldier
Shambel:	Company commander (literally, 'commander of 250')
Basciai:	Junior officer.

sound their *negarits* until war was declared by the emperor. The title *lij,* or son, was a civil rather than a military title, indicating descent from an important man, though in fact a *lij* often commanded a provincial force equivalent to that of a *ras*. *Degiasmacc,* or *degiacc negarit,* governed a large province in the emperor's name, and was beneath a *ras* in status. Some had the privilege of 12 *negarit* drums and were as independent as *rases*. Other *degiasmaccs* were found in the emperor's

immediate retinue. An ordinary *degiacc* governed a smaller area, having been nominated by the emperor or by a *ras*. Many such men came from the minor aristocracy. An ordinary *fitaurari,* (rather than the *First Fitaurari*) traditionally commanded the vanguard of an army, and ranked immediately below the army's commander, who in turn often held the title of *degiacc*. An *asmacc* commanded the rearguard, being beneath a *fitaurari* in rank during wartime, though also governing a district in peace. The *cagnasmacc* commanded the right wing; ranking immediately below the *asmacc,* he was also a district governor in peacetime. The *grasmacc* commanded the left wing, governed a district and was subordinate to the *first grasmacc* in war, though the latter's role remains unclear. The term *scium* meant 'head', and was a title attached to a district, though status and function varied according to local traditions. In Tigre, for example, the *scium* of Tembien ranked between a *degiacc* and a *fitaurari,* whereas the *scium* of Tzera ranked only as a *cagnasmacc*. The term *barambaras* was given to commanders of specialised troops; for example, the *barambaras* of cavalry and the *barambaras* of artillery ranked roughly the same as a *grasmacc*. The term *seleca* meant 'commander of a thousand', and was widely used to indicate a senior soldier, while *shambel* literally meant 'commander of 250' and was approximately equivalent to a company commander. A *basciai* had originally been a junior officer, and reflected earlier Turkish military influence, coming from the Ottoman-Egyptian title of *bashi*. It had also increased in importance, possibly because of Haile Selassie's modernisation of his army.

The Ethiopian regular army was known either as the 'crown army,' or as the *Mahel Safari,* or Army of the Centre, and was distinct from the feudal levies as well as the emperor's new *Zabanga* and Imperial Guard. Until the 1930s its primary function had been internal security rather than external defence, and the formations which existed at the start of Haile Selassie's reign resulted from his earlier struggles with Empress Zauditu. The army's sympathies had generally been with the empress, and its importance had also been undermined by Haile Selassie's increasingly powerful Imperial Guard. Nevertheless, the *Mahel Safari*

Perhaps the most colourful of the Italian army's colonial troops were the 'Penne di Falco' Eritrean cavalry. Here they present arms to Gen. Pirzio-Biroli, commander of the Eritrean colonial division, following the Italian capture of Dese which had been Emperor Haile Selassie's military headquarters.

15

remained a significant military force and in 1934, shortly before the Wal Wal incident, it was given a new banner depicting St George slaying the dragon, a banner also regarded as that of the Ethiopian army as a whole.

Emperor Haile Selassie regarded his Imperial Guard as the nucleus of a modern Ethiopian army, though its first function was to control potentially rebellious *rases*. The Imperial Guard developed from the *Zabanga*, a modern gendarmerie or police for the Addis Ababa area which had been established for Ras Tafari by Swiss military advisers even before his coronation as emperor. Once Ras Tafari became Emperor Haile Selassie the *Zabanga*'s antiquated armament was replaced by Mannlicher rifles purchased in Czechoslovakia and the Swiss were replaced by five Belgian officers led by Major Polet. They converted part of the *Zabanga* into the Imperial Guard, with an infantry battalion, a cavalry squadron and a military band appearing in 1930. These units were sometimes referred to as the *Kebur Zabanga* or Great *Zabanga,* though this term was also applied to the Imperial Guard officer corps.

Four years later the emperor gave the Guard's commander, *Barambaras* Mokria, a new banner portraying the Lion of Judah – the symbol of the Ethiopian ruling dynasty. By that time the Imperial Guard was more than 4,000 strong in the capital alone, with three additional battalions around Harar and others in the process of formation. One infantry battalion included a machine gun company, while the cavalry rode large horses imported from Australia. Around this time a visiting British military attaché described the Imperial Guard as a 'really remarkable' force. In 1935 Asfau Wolde Giorghis, an Ethiopian officer who had graduated from the French Military Academy at St Cyr, was placed in command of the Second Battalion of the Guard and made *Ietor*

ABOVE **Soldiers of the Italian *Regio Corpo di Truppe Coloniali*'s Libyan Brigade. The men in the front rank all appear to be NCOs, some with very long service. Although they wear the distinctive soft fez or *takia* traditionally worn by the urban and coastal peoples of Libya, such units also included Arab volunteers from Yemen and Eritrea.**

BELOW **An Ethiopian feudal levy during a muster between November 1934 and the outbreak of war in 1935. They may be the troops who followed Ras Mulughieta, the Minister of War, or those from the Harar region. Though their clothing and appearance is very mixed, most have rifles and each group has its own flag. (F.D. Corfield photograph, Royal Geographical Society, London)**

Abegaz (military commander) at Saho, where he was ordered to raise a modern provincial army of 6,000 men in the first effort to update Ethiopia's local levies. But Haile Selassie's plans to do the same elsewhere were overtaken by the war.

Many junior officers in the *Zabanga* and Imperial Guard were the sons of traditional military leaders, and several were sent for officer training in Europe. In January 1935 a cadet school was also established in the emperor's summer residences at Oletta, near Addis Ababa, with assistance from a Swedish military mission led by Captain Viking Thamm of the Swedish Royal Life Guards. One hundred and twenty students aged 16 to 20 and who could already speak French, were selected from the élite Tafari Makonnen and Menelik Schools. Most were sons of noblemen and had similar strengths and weaknesses to those seen among military cadets in Egypt. They were highly intelligent, averse to physical exercise, full of confidence, and had a tendency to overestimate their own capabilities. Many had, in fact, been educated in Egypt or France. They were expected to take over from existing Guards officers, many of whom clung to archaic military ideas and tactics. Forty-five students began the infantry training, 25 each attending engineer, cavalry and artillery courses, but war broke out before any course was completed. Other junior officers and NCOs were taught to read and write.

The role of foreign advisers and mercenaries in the modernisation of the Ethiopian armies was crucial. Haile Selassie had turned to Belgium because he did not want to rely on a neighbouring colonial power, and the Belgians also had a fine reputation following the First World War. A new group arrived in 1934, led by Major Dothée and including Captain Listray and Cavalry Lieutenant Le Chevalier de Dieudonnée de Corbeek Overloo. Their first task was to establish a military training centre at Harar where the emperor hoped to create two new infantry battalions, another cavalry squadron, a camel-mounted infantry squadron and a squadron of armoured cars for the Imperial Guard.

As the crisis with Italy deepened, the Belgian government tried to prevent a larger group of volunteers going to Ethiopia in 1935. This group, calling itself the Unofficial Belgian Mission, and led by Colonel Reul, included men with considerable experience in the Belgian Congo. They side-stepped their government's obstructions by wearing their uniforms and medals, but not their Belgian insignia. Unfortunately, the two groups of Belgians did not get on, and sometimes refused to salute each other. Once the war began Colonel Reul and Lieutenant de Fraippont remained in the emperor's headquarters at Dese. Major

Amongst the best-armed men in this same feudal levy was what appears to be a specific unit distinguished by decorated fezes. This suggests that they might have come from the Muslim eastern city of Harar, rather than the Christian highlands of central Ethiopia. (F.D. Corfield photograph, Royal Geographical Society, London)

17

Delery served as a military instructor, Captain Armand Debois and Lieutenant Gustav Witmeur were attached to Ras Nasibu Zemanuel's army in the Ogaden Desert, while Lieutenant Frère and Captain Cambier served with Ras Desta Damtu's army in the Sidamo-Borana areas where Cambier was killed early in the campaign. Relations between these men and the Turkish advisers on the southern front were also tense, with Farouk Bey describing his Belgian colleagues as a bunch of 'lawyers, shop keepers and comedians'. Interestingly enough, all these foreign military advisers were called *Ferenghi* or 'Franks' by the Ethiopians – including the Turks.

The three Turks were among the most experienced foreign advisers in Ethiopian service. They arrived from Istanbul and were promptly sent to advise Ras Nasibu in the largely Muslim city of Harar, replacing Major Dothée who was recalled to Addis Ababa. Their leader, General, Mehmet Wehib Pasha, was described by a British newspaper correspondent as 'an elderly, stout, short man in off-white trousers and gym shoes... a romantic'. Elderly and romantic or not, Mehmet Wehib was a highly skilled soldier whose knowledge was more relevant to the Ethiopians than that of most other advisers. He also had a particular hatred of European imperialism, having fought the Italian invasion of Libya in 1911-12, the British and French at Gallipoli in 1915 (when he commanded the Turkish 2nd Army), the Russians in the Caucasus towards the end of the First World War, where he commanded the 3rd Army, and the Greek invasion of Turkey in 1922-23. Mehmet Wehib Pasha had even refused command of the Ottoman 7th Army in Palestine because he would not serve under a German general. It was General Wehib who designed the fortified positions in front of Harar, which for many months were thought impregnable enough to inhibit Graziani's actions. In fact, Graziani described Wehib Pasha as, 'a man of war with considerable experience of war of movement'. Wehib's fortifications

A group of leading Ethiopian warriors before a feast at the Emperor Haile Selassie's *gibbi* or palace in the 1930s. Shields decorated with gilded filigree were a mark of status or military leadership, but only one of the men in this picture has the lionskin headdress normally associated with a *ras* or ruler of a large province. Other headgear varies considerably, and includes one large white turban, probably indicating that the wearer came from the Ethiopian Empire's many Muslim peoples. (ex-Illustrazione Italiana)

RIGHT **The Court Chamberlain on the steps of the emperor's palace in Addis Ababa on 3 October 1935 announcing an imperial** *Awaj* **or decree ordering a general mobilisation. Behind the Chamberlain a solitary drummer beats the Emperor Haile Selassie's great lion-hide** *negarit* **drum.**

ABOVE **An Ethiopian *ras* or aristocratic governor of a province and leader of a private feudal army, aiming a light machine gun. Normally such powerful modern weapons were kept under the emperor's personal control.**

were not the African Hindenburg Line they seemed, however, but were a huge bluff lacking much barbed wire and weaponry.

The other Turkish advisers were Farouk Bey, described as a tall, thin, military martinet who was placed in charge of administration, and Tarik Bey, 'a black man with a short moustache…, a pure Sudanese…, well over fifty.'.

A larger military mission consisted of Swedes led by General Virgin. Though they were not officially seconded by their government, Sweden paid their salaries. These men restructured the Imperial Guard and designed new uniforms for Haile Selassie's palace staff. More significantly, they also tried to teach the Ethiopians modern ideas of deployment and guerrilla warfare, but on 28 September 1935, five days before the Italian invasion, General Virgin left, suffering from altitude sickness. Their efforts were most noticeable on the northern front where there was some improvement in Ethiopian fortifications and communication.

As the crisis developed in 1935, trains from Djibouti in French-Somaliland brought ammunition and weapons, together with an increasing number of journalists, photographers, doctors, missionaries, missionaries, adventurers, mercenaries and arms dealers. They came from Europe, Asia and America, and included idealists ranging from anti-Fascists, to Nazis and pacifists – the latter mostly being sent to help various Red Cross organisations under the Greek military doctor, Lieutenant Colonel Arussi, who was already resident in Addis Ababa. Others were colourful characters such as a pair of Irish adventurers called Brophil and Hicket, a retired English Master of Foxhounds named Major Gerald Burgoyne, a former French NCO of Armenian origin recruited to help bridge the cultural gap between Belgians and Ethiopians, and a Russian electrical engineer named Theodore Konovaloff who had previously worked in Turkey and Egypt. Then there was the Swiss Major Wittlin who thought he was going to command troops in the Awash area, but ended up in charge of an Oerlikon anti-aircraft battery defending a vital bridge over the Awash River on the Addis Ababa–Djibouti railway line. A Cuban aviator or airgunner named Captain

Alessandro del Valle became Ras Mulughieta's personal machine gunner on the northern front, but perhaps the strangest to modern readers was an Austrian doctor named Schuppler. He had taken part in the failed Nazi *putsch* in 1934 and hated Mussolini because the Italian dictator had defended Austrian independence from a German take-over. Most of these mercenaries and advisers fled Ethiopia even before the final battle of Maych'ew, though the Russian Konovaloff and the Turks remained to the end.

Ras Mulughieta, the Ethiopian *First Fitaurari* or Minister of War from November 1934 to the fall of Addis Ababa in spring 1936, with his personal guards. They are largely dressed in traditional garb, but are armed with modern rifles. Ras Mulughieta himself had very traditional views, particularly on warfare, and was said to regard all Europeans as 'friends of Italy'.

The most unsatisfactory mercenaries were found among the pilots who volunteered to fly Ethiopia's tiny air force, though there were idealists among them. They included Count Carl von Rosen, stunt pilot and the black sheep of his family, who brought an air ambulance to Addis Ababa just before the Italian invasion. He flew many mercy missions, carrying medical supplies and wounded men until his aircraft was hit on the ground by Italian fighters. Von Rosen escaped, but over 30 years later he was killed, again on the ground, when his little piston-engined bomber operating in support of Biafran secessionists in Nigeria was hit by an Egyptian MiG-17 reconnaissance pilot named Nabil Shuwakri. Another loyal pilot was Lieutenant Micha Babitcheff, a

Gen. Graziani wearing a light coloured solar-topee, at a field radio-station on the southern front. Graziani was a very cautious commander who spent most of his career in colonial service. His brutal crushing of Libyan resistance made him hated throughout the Arab world, and in 1941 he was defeated by Gen. Wavell in Egypt. Yet his loyalty to Mussolini rarely wavered, and after the Second World War Graziani was imprisoned for five years.

Russian adventurer who directed the Ethiopian air force until most of its planes were destroyed. Count Hilaire du Berrier tried to raise a volunteer flying corps in Europe and was eventually captured by the Italians 55km from Addis Ababa, the day before the Ethiopian capital fell. Most of the other Frenchmen who had kept the Ethiopian air force flying since 1928 left before the Italian invasion. But Corriger remained for a while, against his government's orders, and secretly flew Haile Selassie on a tour of the main military bases before leaving for Djibouti on 30 November 1935. The mechanic Demeaux stayed until the final fall of Addis Ababa to the Italians. A German named Ludwig Weber arrived via the Sudan, and flew the emperor's personal plane, only to be killed during the chaotic fall of Addis Ababa. Some pilots arrived with no money at all, including a black American named Colonel Hubert Fauntleroy Julian who called himself the 'Black Eagle of Harlem'. Like a fellow black American, Johannes Robinson from Chicago, Julian felt ethnic solidarity with the Ethiopians, but unfortunately crashed one of Haile Selassie's few serviceable aircraft. Most of these pilots were given Ethiopian officer rank, but some were little more than cheats. According to Emilio Faldella, the Italian Information Centre in Cairo received a strange proposal in February 1936, purporting to come from a Frenchman named Drouillet who had been sent to Europe to collect a Beechcraft aeroplane. He supposedly offered to kidnap Haile Selassie and fly him to Asmara, capital of Italian Eritrea, in return for a large sum of money.

How much impact these foreigners had on the Ethiopian resistance remains a matter of debate. Some historians claim that it was their training and guidance which enabled the Ethiopians to halt the initial Italian thrusts on the northern front. Others suggest that a significant number, even including Theodore Konovaloff, were in Italian pay. The mercenary pilots clearly had almost no effect, but the Ethiopian air force was too small and ill-equipped to do more than ferry senior officers, munitions and medical supplies around the country.

Ethiopian Uniforms and Equipment

The only Ethiopian forces who consistently wore uniforms were the *Zabanga* and its offshoot, the Imperial Guard. Many officers of the *Mahel Safari* purchased khaki European-style uniforms and solar-topees, while some soldiers in the regular *Mahel Safari* also had khaki clothing and broad-brimmed grey hats. Many of these individuals were ex-members of Italian

Italian soldiers of the motorised 30th Infantry Division Sabauda which formed part of the 1st Army Corps on the northern front. This Corps, under Gen. Santini, was on the extreme left flank of the Italian line and fought its way from Adigrat on the Eritrean frontier to Haile Selassie's headquarters at Dese. Note the presence of a civilian in the lower right-hand corner, perhaps a driver. The name GONDRAN stencilled on the side of the lorry is the trademark of a private company involved in building roads for the Italian army.

Vehicles of the 30th Infantry Division Sabauda, 1st Army Corps, negotiating a narrow road on the northern front. Existing tracks were hardly suitable for large numbers of motorised vehicles and could have provided the Ethiopians with vulnerable targets if their commanders had attempted the guerrilla strategy advocated by Haile Selassie. But they did not do so until after the official war was over. It is worth noting that the first three trucks are all of different makes; the leading vehicle being a British-made Bedford.

colonial forces or of the British King's African Rifles, all of whom were called *Tripoloc* and who may have retained part of their old uniforms.

The uniforms of the Imperial Guard were distinguished by coloured collar-patches for various branches of service: red for riflemen, dark green for machine gunners, black for artillery, blue for cavalry and sky blue for radio-telegraphists. The same system, though with different colours, was used by the Italians, Egyptians and Turks. Imperial Guard officers were distinguished from all others by having pieces of lionskin attached to their caps and epaulettes. Though the Imperial Guard drilled in a European manner and were basically dressed in European style, their lack of boots was comparable to that of other more traditional parts of the Ethiopian army. In fact the emperor banned boots on the grounds that they weakened an Ethiopian's ability to cross rough terrain.

Ethiopian feudal retinues and levies wore traditional costume consisting of toga-like *shammas* and the jodhpur-like trousers which had been introduced in the 19th century. During the early stages of the Italian invasion many warriors dyed these white garments a muddy or ochre colour to make themselves less visible. Many men also wore broad sun-hats made from raffia or dried grass. Europeans found it very difficult to identify members of a particular feudal force by their clothing, although there were regional variations. Much the same applied to distinctions of rank, other than the deference shown by juniors to seniors. On the other hand distinctively clad units included the *First Fitaurari*'s personal band of hornblowers dressed in European style, and his scarlet-turbaned drummers rode mules. Despite his own traditional views and his distrust of foreigners, Ras Mulughieta sometimes wore a khaki uniform instead of a traditional lionskin trimmed cloak.

Ethiopian weaponry varied hugely in type and age. The emperor had wanted the whole army equipped with Belgian weapons, and all Imperial Guardsmen had rifles, though some were old French Lebels. *Rases* were largely responsible for arming their own followers, and as tension mounted old guns sold for enormous sums in Addis Ababa. Soft-nosed bullets which caused horrific injuries were used by many Ethiopian soldiers during the subsequent campaign, although these were not the internationally banned dumdums, merely the bullets used in antiquated weapons. Ethiopian raids on Italian supply lines also gathered additional machine guns and their ammunition, while the Imperial Guard's mortar-teams became very proficient by the end of the war.

Ethiopian artillery was even more varied. Heavier weapons were traditionally kept under the emperor's personal control until the emergence of Ras Tafari's modern army in the 1920s and 1930s when they began to be found in provincial garrisons. Even so the most modern weapons were still retained in the Imperial *Gemgiabiet,* or military warehouses, controlled by Haile Selassie's *Cagnasmacc* Wolde Johannes. Most field guns had been captured from the Italians at Adwa in 1886 and their ranges were unknown to most Ethiopian commanders. Since then, a steady, if limited, flow of more up-to-date weapons meant that by 1933 the Ethiopians had around 220 artillery pieces, with some 400 rounds, though these included obsolete bronze cannon. In addition, there were six Stokes mortars. Colt and Führer machine guns included around 250 heavy and 800 lighter weapons, along with 175 modern Browning machine guns. Several important weapons orders were outstanding when, in July 1935, the suppliers abrogated their contracts because of the worsening crisis. Skoda of Czechoslovakia refused to deliver artillery, Denmark cancelled a mixed order, and only Belgium completed its contract for cartridges. On the other hand Germany, still smarting from Mussolini's defence of Austria from a Nazi take-over, sold Ethiopia a dozen modern Pak 35/36 anti-tank weapons. When the war began Ethiopia was believed to have 234 artillery pieces, including old bronze cannons, and a larger number of Stokes mortars. The most publicised weapons were Oerlikon light anti-aircraft guns which Emperor Haile Selassie himself fired at Italian aircraft. Later in the war they were also used against ground targets.

ABOVE **Men of the élite Italian *Alpini,* probably the 5th Alpine Division Pusteri, in action at the battle of Amba Aradam on the northern front. Here, a large Ethiopian force under Ras Mulughieta took up a position from which it could threaten the fortified Italian base-camp at Mek'ele.**

BELOW **Eritrean *askaris,* mostly wearing *bustina* side-caps like those of metropolitan Italian troops, dancing before or after a battle. At least two soldiers, including the man in the centre, carry traditional curved sabres.**

Organisation and Tactics

Ethiopian forces still relied on mules, and in some areas, camels for transport. Such pack-animals also carried the sacks of dried peas which formed the basic food of more prosperous Ethiopian warriors, while boy servants carried the warriors' weapons. In fact the success of Belgian military advisers in getting Ethiopian regular soldiers to carry their own gear in haversacks was regarded as a major achievement which led to greater mobility and fewer camp followers.

The trumpeter of a squadron of 'Penne di Falco' Eritrean cavalry, sounding the muster. This picture was probably taken when the men were reviewed by Gen. Pirzio-Biroli, commander of the Eritrean Corps on the northern front, following their capture of Dese.

Ethiopia's lack of motorised vehicles was hardly surprising since the only modern roads ran from Addis Ababa to Dese, from Addis Ababa to Sidamo with a planned extension to the Kenyan border, and part of the way from Addis Ababa to Harar. The numbers of vehicles available to the army in 1935 remains unclear as additional material reached the country in the immediate build-up to the war. It probably included around seven armed (but unarmoured) Fiat 'assault cars,' seven or so Ford Type A and other lorries mounting machine guns, and perhaps seven so-called armoured cars. The latter may have been confused with the armed truck or 'assault cars', since other reports maintained that the Ethiopians only had one real armoured car. Some of these vehicles would be used in the Ogaden.

Ethiopian military communications were terrible, and it often took days for news to reach Addis Ababa from the front. Several runners were also intercepted by Italian soldiers or their sympathisers, yet this remained the main form of Ethiopian military communication. Imitation bird calls were also used on at least one battlefield. The only Ethiopian radio station was located at Akaki airfield, south-west of the capital, while the army's few radio sets were so easily intercepted and decoded that they provided the Italians with information about all major Ethiopian troop movements.

The Ethiopian army's medical services were equally rudimentary, with a small and hopelessly overburdened staff. However, international sympathy brought official Red Cross ambulance units from Sweden, Britain, Holland, Egypt and Finland. One of the most important was the Egyptian which was, strictly speaking, a Red Crescent unit. Like their British Red Cross colleagues, the Egyptian doctors and ambulances were bombed by Italian aircraft despite highly visible Red Cross signs. Unfortunately, the Swiss doctor in overall charge of these volunteers spent much of his time soothing the injured pride of the Ethiopian Army Medical Corps.

The Ethiopian air force was not run solely by foreigners. It was based at Akaki and, by 1935, had 12 aircraft with around a hundred ten kg bombs. Only three machines were fully operational, three being of limited value, three described as useless, and the remaining number unaccounted for. They included four Potez 25 two-seater reconnaissance aircraft bought in 1927, which lacked guns, ammunition and were in need of complete overhaul. Two Fokker monoplanes were in good condition, but lacked spares. The other aircraft consisted of a Junkers trimotor, a Farman monoplane, a little Breda sports plane, a 12-seater Beechcraft, which may have arrived during the course of the war, and a little monoplane called the *Ethiopia I*. This was basically a rebuilt and greatly modified De Havilland Moth, constructed at Akaki under the direction of Haile Selassie's personal pilot Ludwig Weber. It is now preserved in the Italian Air Force Museum at Vigna di Valle. One Potez 25

1: Officer of the Kebur Zabagna,
Ethiopian Imperial Guard
2: Officer in the Mahel Safari,
regular Ethiopian Army
3: Selfegna, ordinary soldier of the
Mahel Safari regular Ethiopian Army

A

1: Embilta player
2: Amharic Gascegna, traditional warrior
3: Galla cavalryman

B

1: Askari of the IX Arab-Somali Battalion RCTC, Somalia
2: Capo, Banda Dubat, Sergeant RCTC, Somalia
3: Bulucbasci of the Camel-Mounted Artillery, Sergeant RCTC, Somalia

1

2

3

C

1: Cavalry Askari of the 'Penne di Falco' (Hawk Feathers), RCTC, Eritrea
2: Jusbasci Capo, Zaptie, RCTC, Eritrea
3: Muntaz, XIV Eritrean Battalion, Corporal RCTC, Eritrea

1: Infantry Corporal, 60th Calabria Regiment, Sila Division
2: Vice Capo Squadra Ardito, MVSN
3: Corporal Major, 3rd Bersaglieri Regiment, Colonna Celere

ASMARA
(ERITREA)

D.I.A.0
F.A. 039

E

1: Primo Capo Squadra (Sergeant Major), MVSN
2: Infantry Tenente (Lieutenant), 63rd Cagliari Regiment, Assiette Division
3: Milite, 221st 'Italiani all'Estero Legion', 6th Tevere Division, MVSN

F

1: Milite, III Centuria Lavoratori, MVSN
2: Capitano, XLV Eritrean Battalion, RCTC, Eritrea
3: Alpino, 11th Regiment, Pusteria Division

G

1: Pilot Capitano, Regia Aeronautica
2: Pilot Capitano of the 15th 'La Disperata' Squadron in flying gear
3: Askari, VIII Libyan Infantry Battalion, Libia Division

also survived the war. The Ethiopian government had recently ordered the construction of several provincial airfields, but none were complete and the air force also suffered from an acute shortage of technically trained personnel. Foreign mercenary pilots remained important, though six Ethiopian pilots had completed training before war broke out, one of whom had passed with an 'excellent' grade. They alone flew the Potez 25s and sadly featured as villains in a work of popular fiction set in post-1936 Portuguese East Africa. This was written by a British author who regarded the existence of black pilots as a threat to the white man's status in Africa (Wilfred Robinson, *The Black Planes*, London 1938; illustrated by Jack Nicolle). The Turkish adviser, Gen. Mehmet Wehib, had been hoping to establish a system of air-cover for Ethiopian defences around Harar but this came to nothing.

At the start of the war Ethiopian morale was very high. The troops' fathers and grandfathers had, after all, defeated the Italians at Adwa. Ethiopian troops had an offensive spirit and highly developed sense of mockery as shown by their mimicking of Italian bugle calls at the Ende Pass where they trapped a column of Italian troops for a while. They were also extremely keen on plunder, and a tradition of taking the genitals of slain enemies persisted, particularly among Galla auxiliaries. The Ethiopians tended to be warriors rather than workers, however, and this limited their effectiveness in prolonged or defensive warfare. The Italians' high opinion of Ethiopian soldiers may also have been a hangover from Adwa, since other outsiders maintained that the courage of Ethiopian warriors was found in a crowd rather than as individuals. They were virtually unstoppable in a massed charge, but were also prone to panic. A defeated Ethiopian commander could expect to be flogged, particularly if he lost much military equipment, and if an Ethiopian leader was killed or wounded the morale of his followers frequently collapsed. It was a terrible disgrace for a leader's body to fall into enemy hands, which was why the corpse of *Bitwoded* Makonnen, commander of an army in the Wollo area, was cut in half and hidden in two *negarit* war drums so that it could be taken home for proper burial. There were

Somali *dubats* or irregulars manning a machine gun position on the southern front. These Muslim soldiers fought with considerable ferocity against their traditional Christian Ethiopian foes, having at least one massacre by Emperor Haile Selassie's men to avenge.

similarly cases where *negarit* drums were buried to stop them being captured by the Italians. On at least one occasion drums were even given a funeral by an Ethiopian priest.

In the opinion of the Italian General Badoglio, the modernisation of the Ethiopian army was largely superficial, with leadership remaining in the hands of aristocratic *rases* or churchmen, many of whom tended to be irresolute, as well as old-fashioned. Staff organisation was rudimentary, and tactics were

based on massed frontal attacks rather than the guerrilla warfare advocated by Emperor Haile Selassie. Large forces assembled on the Ogaden front appeared capable of invading Italian Somalia, but did not do so, perhaps having been put off by Graziani's pre-emptive advance. Ethiopian regulars and levies could, however, move with astonishing speed across the roughest country. On the march they tended to use numerous tracks rather than a single route, with a small advance guard sent ahead. There was little obvious order, but the men sorted themselves out quickly, even though foreign observers could rarely tell how. At first there were no precautions against air attack, and in camp the soldiers bunched around their leaders with small outposts established a short distance away in the direction of the enemy.

In battle, the men fought around their own leaders, the main tactical unit ranging from 1,000 to 3,000 men. On the march and in battle, instructions were passed from the commander to his immediate subordinates and so on down to those in command of individual units. The senior commander's troops were almost invariably placed at the centre of a battle line, with the overall battle formation having a centre, two wings, vanguard and rearguard. This mirrored medieval Middle Eastern practice almost exactly, and showed where Ethiopian military traditions originated. Battlefield tactics consisted of a massed charge, repeated as often as possible or necessary, and Ethiopian troops were highly effective in close combat, especially at night. The tradition of relying on one great day-long battle to decide the outcome of a war remained strong among the *rases*. There were, in fact, several occasions when Ethiopian troops, having achieved a tactical success on the first day, retired the following night rather than repeating their attacks for a second day.

Traditionalism similarly influenced Ethiopian attitudes towards field fortifications. When the Russian adviser Theodore Konovaloff was sent north shortly before war broke out, he found that the few Ethiopian trenches were too shallow and mostly in the wrong places. In reply to Konovaloff's criticisms, the local *ras* said, 'What sort of war is this, fighting behind stones?' Some Ethiopian regulars learned to make tank-traps and proper entrenchments during the course of the war, but the only real fortified positions were those built by Ras Nesibu's forces under Gen. Mehmet Wehib's direction near Sassabaneh, south-east of Harar.

THE ITALIAN ARMY

The Italian army appeared to undergo many changes between the First and Second World Wars, but some were superficial and reflected the Fascist dictator Mussolini's use of the armed forces as propaganda weapons. The army had the potential to be a large force, since all Italian men over 18 were liable for call-up. The first 18 months were spent as full-time national service conscripts. Men then underwent regular post-service training until the age of 33, after which they remained reservists until 54. The training of reservists was, however, rudimentary.

The structure of the Italian Royal Army, as distinct from the Fascist Militia (see below), had changed little, though Benito Mussolini had taken over most of King Victor Emmanuel III's military responsibilities.

Ethiopian Regular Forces 1935

Imperial Guard:
12 machine gun sections
3 companies of heavy machine guns
1 mortar unit
1 squadron cavalry
3 batteries of mule-artillery
1 platoon radio telegraphists
1 medical section
1 band

Air Force:
12 aircraft based at Akaki

Mahel Safari provincial units:
Amino
Gubba
Gurage
Jima
Mui
Om Hajer
Sela
Sodo
Wollega

'Modernised' feudal regional forces under loyal *rases*:
Bal
Harar
Sidamo-Borana
Wollo
Saho
Illub Abor

Unmodernised feudal levies existed in every other part of the Ethiopian Empire.

RIGHT **Italian Marine Infantry of the San Marco Battalion clearing a road. Like almost all Italian soldiers involved in the invasion of Ethiopia, these men from the Venice region spent a great deal of time clearing tracks and making new roads. As a result the Italian army was able to make use of its large number of trucks and armoured vehicles. The men in this picture have Battaglione San Marco written on cloth bands across their solar topees.**

ABOVE **Though *dubat* frontier auxiliaries in Italian colonial service were Muslims, as were all Somalis, those working for the Italian medical corps still wore a Red Cross on their turbans. Note the camouflaged medical tent in the background.**

Nevertheless, the king remained the army's nominal commander-in-chief. Beneath Mussolini was the *Commando Supremo* consisting of a military staff which operated through the Ministries of War, Admiralty and Air to various regional high commands. One of the latter was responsible for the Italian East African territories of Eritrea and Somalia. The army itself was divided into infantry, *celere* or mobile, motorised, and armoured divisions which remained the basic administrative and tactical formations. Within them, only a few units were up to strength in men or equipment, while frontier guards and colonial troops recruited from indigenous populations were organised separately, as were irregular *Dubats* or Somali frontier auxiliaries. Army ranks included some which had no direct parallels in the British army.

Uniforms

Rank badges were worn on headgear as well as shoulder-straps or forearms, though not on both. The MVSN Fascist Militia (see below), however, sometimes wore rank-badges on both shoulders and cuffs. They also distinguished themselves by wearing a black cummerbund, with or without a black shirt, when not wearing a tunic. Unit or arm-of-service badges were placed on most forms of headgear, while the colour of collar-patches indicated the same thing. Metallic divisional 'arm shields' had been introduced in 1934, and were supposedly worn on the left sleeve by all soldiers, although this was not always the case.

Italian army uniforms had traditionally been serviceable and comfortable until the introduction of a stiff high collar in 1909. Fortunately, this was replaced in 1934 by a soft collar and tie such as those already worn by the famous *Arditi* commandos in World War One. The main difference between the uniforms of officers and other ranks was that officers wore a lighter twill fabric. A new tropical field tunic for NCOs and other ranks was designed for the Ethiopian campaign, based upon advice from the Corps of Colonial Troops. It was basically the same as the ordinary uniform, but was made from light khaki linen. During the Ethiopian winter months, officers wore a darker khaki tunic similar to that worn in Italy. When not wearing a tunic, officers often wore a broad khaki cummerbund over the shirt; this comfortable way of spreading the weight of a belt and other kit in hot climates had been used for centuries by Middle Eastern soldiers. During the Ethiopian conflict, many troops, above all officers, adopted the light and comfortable *Sahariana* bush-jacket which had first been introduced for troops serving in Libya. It was such an excellent garment, that it was subsequently adopted by many of Rommel's Afrika Korps.

Italian soldiers were otherwise characterised by very baggy trousers, khaki-olive coloured versions having been introduced for NCOs and other ranks for the Ethiopian campaign. They

ITALIAN RANK AND CORPS INSIGNIA

1 Infantry brass badge for a cork helmet, placed over the national cockade (see Plate E1).

2 *Bersaglieri* brass badge for a cork helmet (see plate E3).

3 Colonial infantry brass badge (see plate G2). It is the same as that worn by Libyan infantry, but without the national cockade (see plate H3).

4 *Alpini* black embroidered badge (see plate G3).

5 *Carabinieri* and *Zaptie* brass badge (see plate D2).

6 Camel-mounted artillery brass badge (see plate C3) with rank insignia stars for a *Bulucbasci Capo*.

7 MVSN brass badge for a cork helmet, worn without a national cockade (see plates F1 & F3).

8 MVSN *bustina* (side-cap) badge (see plate E2).

9 MVSN Workers' Century brass badge for a cork helmet with black cloth cockade (see plate G1).

10 MVSN Black Shirt Division brass arm badge painted black (see plate E2; plate F3 has a comparable badge made of cloth).

11 Infantry Division brass arm badge painted green.

12 Regia Aeronautica 15th 'La Disperata' Bombardamento Terrestre Squadron badge (see plate H2).

13 Infantry regiment cloth *mostrina* collar badge (see plate E1).

14 *Bersaglieri* and *Alpini fiamma* cloth badge, crimson for *Bersaglieri* and green for *Alpini* (see plate E3).

15 MVSN cloth collar badge (see plates E2 & F3).

16 Colonial infantry shoulder-straps for officers, corps and rank insignia stars, displayed with native battalion colours in cloth stripes around the collar straps.

17 Army NCO rank insignia; black cloth for a *corporal major* (17a) and embroidered gold for a *sergènte* (17b).

proved very comfortable in hot climates, and were tucked into boots to protect a man's legs from thorns and insects. In Ethiopia khaki puttees or brown leather leggings also protected the legs. Officers were permitted to wear shorts, though other ranks also did so on occasions. The high, tan-coloured boots of NCOs and other ranks gave additional protection in scrubby terrain. Boots worn by officers were also brown, unlike the black worn in Italy, and included lighter elastic-sided versions. Sandals were mostly worn by local troops or *askaris*, but were also used by some Italian soldiers, particularly those involved in heavy labour.

The distinctive *bustina* side-cap was supposed to replace a peaked cap on active service, along with the 1933 model steel helmet. Rather old-fashioned wide-brimmed pith or cork sun-helmets were issued for service in the colonies and would become a characteristic part of Italian colonial uniform. Those issued to officers had a flatter crown, but many purchased their own in a number of different styles. Even more striking headgear included the grey-green brimmed felt hats of the *Alpini*, with a crow's feather for NCOs and other ranks, an eagle's

Italian Military Ranks

Ufficiali: Officers

Marshal of the Empire	
Marshal of Italy	
Maresciallo:	Field Marshal (see also Maresciallo: senior warrant officer)
Generale:	General of the Army
Generale:	of a Corps (two grades)
Tenente Generale:	Lieutenant General (Artillery, engineers & technical branches only)
Major Generale	(Artillery, engineers & technical branches only)
Colonello:	Colonel
Tenente Colonnello:	Lieutenant-Colonel
Maggiore:	Major
Primo Capitano:	First Captain
Capitano:	Captain (including Chaplains)
Primo Tenente:	First Lieutenant
Sotto Tenente:	Second Lieutenant (including Band Leaders)
Officer Cadet	

Sottufficiali: NCOs

Maresciallo:	Senior Warrant Officer, in three Classes (see also Maresciallo: Field Marshal)
Sergente Maggiore:	Sergeant-Major
Brigadiere:	Sergeant-Major (Carabinieri & Guardia di Finanza
Sergente:	Sergeant
Corporal-Major:	Senior Corporal

Truppa: Other Ranks

Corporal	(equivalent to US Army Private First Class)
Private	

Colonial force NCOs

Jusbasci:	Warrant Officer
Bulucbasci:	Sergeant
Muntaz:	Corporal

Dubat Somali irregulars

Capo Comandante:	Warrant Officer
Capo:	Sergeant
Sotto-Capo:	Corporal

feather for officers and a goose feather for generals. The soft red Zouave-style fez with a blue tassel of the élite *bersaglieri* light infantry was an off-duty headgear, whereas the *berseglieri*'s better-known bunch of cockerel feathers was worn on sun-helmets and even steel helmets.

Organisation, Weapons and Equipment

The basic Italian army infantry division consisted of a headquarters, two infantry regiments, sometimes with an additional reserve infantry battalion, plus a mortar battalion, a divisional artillery regiment, a pack-artillery company and an engineer battalion. Each infantry regiment had three rifle battalions, though there could be more, with its own heavy machine guns, light machine guns, light and medium mortars, and light artillery. Some infantry divisions were designated as mountain warfare units, though they were not *Alpini*. Since they were intended to operate in rough terrain, all their artillery was in horse-drawn wagons or was carried by pack animals. The élite *Alpini* themselves were recruited from mountainous parts of Italy, not only the Alpine north, and were among the best troops in the world when it came to operating artillery in the mountains. Their divisions differed from those of the infantry in having their artillery, engineers and other support formations permanently attached, so they were equally experienced in mountain warfare. *Alpini* units were also largely self-supporting. Italy's other infantry élite were the *bersaglieri* who were usually attached to motorised divisions. Each *bersaglieri* light infantry

An Italian CV 3/33 light tank in Ethiopia. This version was armed with a single machine gun and had a crew of two. The tank shown here has the name *Adua* on the side, not to commemorate the catastrophic Italian defeat by the Ethiopians at Adwa in 1896 but as a call for vengeance.

regiment normally consisted of a headquarters company, a motor cycle company and two battalions with support units.

The basic Italian infantry weapon was the Mannlicher-Carcano Model 1891 rifle. This single bolt-action weapon was, however, old-fashioned, and there were many complaints about its performance. Nor could its clip of six rounds be enlarged. Many ordinary troops, as well as officers, carried pistols of varying manufacture. The Model 30 (Breda) machine gun used the same ammunition as the Carcano rifle but, because of the lubricating oil which smoothed the passage of its cartridges, was very easily clogged by dust or sand. The Model 14 (Fiat-Revelli) was a First World War weapon which also used oil-lubricated cartridges. It was heavy, complicated, under-powered and had a low rate of fire. As a result, both the Model 30 and the Model 14 were extremely unpopular. In contrast, the 81mm Mortar Model 35, the Italian army's standard medium infantry support weapon, was excellent in mountains, but was not much used in the desert. The light 45mm Mortar Model 35 was also highly effective and easy to transport, but suffered from an inferior bomb. Italian grenades relied almost entirely on blast and morale effect, with minimal fragmentation.

The artillery regiment within an infantry division had two howitzer batteries and a horse-drawn field battery. Reliance on horse transport would prove a great weakness during the Second World War, but did not seem to be so in Ethiopia. The guns themselves were antiquated and of relatively light calibre. For example the 65/17 infantry support field gun was an obsolete version of the old 65mm mountain gun. Though accurate, easily dismantled and carried by mules, it suffered from inadequate range.

Celere, or mobile, divisions were basically the old cavalry formations which had to some extent been mechanised. They were intended to act in a support or reconnaissance role where firepower was sacrificed for mobility. Each *celere* division consisted of two cavalry regiments, a *bersaglieri* light infantry regiment on bicycles, a *bersaglieri* company on motor cycles, an anti-tank company, a divisional artillery regiment, a light tank group and a company of engineers. The light tank group itself included a headquarters with nine tanks and four squadrons each of 13 tanks. The success of the *celere* divisions during the Ethiopian campaign subsequently led to complacency and they would prove extremely vulnerable during the Second World War.

Italian armoured divisions again only had light tanks in a single tank regiment consisting of three battalions, each theoretically with 55 tanks. The division also had an artillery regiment, a divisional

A Lancia 17 Type 2 armoured car. These had been in service with the Italian army since the First World War, through the civil disturbances of the 1920s and were still in use during the invasion of Ethiopia. Though now out-of-date, the Lancia remained a serviceable machine which packed a considerable punch against Ethiopian feudal levies.

support battalion, an engineer company and a regiment of *bersaglieri* light infantry. The disastrous failure of Italian armour during the North African campaign against the British five years later has tended to mask the fact that the Italian army was the first to use motor vehicles on a large scale. This occurred during the invasion of Libya when the Italian army had a number of armoured trucks. In

Feudal levies, almost certainly from the dominant Amharan peoples of the central highlands of the Ethiopian Empire. They were photographed in autumn 1935, probably during the first few days of the Italian invasion, and had recently been issued with modern rifles.

1918 the Italians purchased French Renault light tanks and made their own version, the Fiat 3000 or Carro Armato M21, which remained in use for many years. Mussolini established the Italian army's first tank regiment in 1927. Four years later, Fiat and Ansaldo jointly produced a light tank, or more accurately an armoured machine gun carrier, similar to the British Carden Lloyd Mk. VI. Two versions were designated CV 3/33 and CV 3/35; the first figure indicating the vehicle's weight, the second the year of introduction. The CV 3/33 had one machine gun and the CV 3/35 two, though the second weapon could be replaced by a flame-thrower, a small bridging device or a smoke dispenser. They were built in large numbers and had a maximum speed of just over 40 mph, with armour between 5mm and 15mm thick.

Italy assembled a large number of other vehicles for the Ethiopian campaign from a variety of sources. They were extremely valuable, but their very diversity caused maintenance problems. They included Italian, British and American transports, among them 100 tracked vehicles from Caterpillar and 450 lorries from Ford. Both vehicles and baggage animals were vital in the Italian–Ethiopian war. For example, huge quantities of water had to be provided: the Libya Division used 80,000 litres of filtered water and 16 cubic metres of purified drinking water on 4 March 1936 alone.

Most of the Italian army's *Regio Corpo Truppe Coloniali* (colonial regiments) were poorly equipped and their training very old-fashioned. Nevertheless, their morale was high and their readiness adequate for the invasion of Ethiopia. Colonial forces' uniforms were also different to those of Italian metropolitan or home units. For example, a broad sash identified arm of service among East African *askaris*, a concept perhaps inherited from the Egyptian forces which garrisoned much of the Eritrean and Somali coast before the Italians arrived. The patterned cloth wound around the tall *tarbusc* or fez of Italian East African cavalry, similarly recalled something almost identical worn by early 19th century Ottoman Turkish cavalry, though here any connection seems too distant to be real. The rank badges worn by colonial forces were much larger than those of metropolitan troops, and also included stars to indicate length of service. The small pieces of lionskin worn by Eritrean *askari* NCOs on their uniforms mirrored those of Ethiopian Imperial Guard

officers. The Dubats whose name meant 'white turbans', were irregular frontier forces first recruited in Somalia by Colonel Bechi, and considerably increased in number during the Italian-Ethiopian War. They wore the traditional Somali *fute*, two strips of cloth across the shoulders and around the body which were sometimes dyed khaki. Rank was indicated by lanyards with tassels around the neck, rather than by badges as in regular forces: green indicated a *capo Commandante* or warrant officer, red a *capo* or sergeant, and black a *sotto-capo*, or corporal. Most Dubats also carried a *billao* or traditional Somali dagger.

The Italian garrison fort at Hobyo (Obbia) in Somaliland, decked with Italian flags. The Sultan of Hobyo had been a loyal ally of the Italians since 1888 and his private army took part in the invasion of Ethiopia on the southern front.

Fascist Militia

The Fascist *Milizia Volontaria Per La Sicurezza Nazionale* (MVSN), or 'Black Shirts' as they were commonly known, was formed in 1922 by Benito Mussolini. Initially the MVSN was recruited from disgruntled ex-servicemen who operated as Fascist bully boys. Mussolini himself was Commander of the MVSN, though a separate chief-of-staff had everyday control, and in time of war the MVSN was placed under the operational command of the Italian Royal Army. The structure of the MVSN supposedly reflected that of the ancient Roman army; units being called a *Zona* (division), *Gruppo* (brigade), *Legion* (regiment), *Cohorte* (battalion), *Centuria* (company), *Manipolo* (platoon) or *Squadra* (section). Some officer ranks also had ancient Roman titles, including the *Console* in charge of a *Legion*, and the *Centurione* in command of a *Centuria*. Normally a MVSN *Legion* consisted of three *Cohorts* which themselves had three *Centuries*. Though in most respects organised like army units, the MVSN *Legions* and their respective parts were smaller than army regiments.

MVSN militiamen were aged from 21 to 36, supported by territorial reservists up to the age of 55. They suffered from an inferiority complex in relation to the army, though the poor quality of MVSN units was not usually the fault of ordinary members. These Black Shirts were, in fact, part-timers often led by second-rate officers with limited military experience. As the Ethiopian War approached, the Italian government decided to draw together the best elements of this huge organisation so that they could fight alongside the regular army. Consequently much of the pseudo-Roman paraphernalia was abandoned. The Colonial Militia was also restructured, eventually consisting of some *Legions* based in Libya, a *Cohort* in Eritrea, a *Manipolo* and a *Squadra* in Somalia, and a *Century*

MVSN Ranks

Lugotente Generale:	equivalent of an Army Corps General.
Console Generale:	equivalent of a Brigade General.
Console:	commander of a Legion.
Centurione:	commander of a Century.
Primo Capo Squadra:	equivalent of a Sergeant-Major.
Vice Capo Squadra:	equivalent of a Corporal-Major.

in the Italian Aegean islands. An additional *Cohort* of volunteers known as the 6th Machine Gunner School was established specially for the Ethiopian war, being drawn from the University Militia and attached to the Tevere *zona* or division. Seven MVSN divisions were ultimately raised for the Ethiopian campaign and were given names commemorating dates in Fascist history. Like army divisions, they were also identified by arm shields.

In order to encourage individual competition and morale, MVSN militiamen from one area were kept together in territorial units like the British regimental system. This, however, resulted in devastating local losses when casualties were high, just as happened to British 'Pals' battalions during the Great War.

The morale of the Italian regular army was high during the Ethiopian War since the Italian public largely supported the invasion. Yet it suffered from wide variations in standards of equipment and training. This was most obvious when comparing élite *bersaglieri* and *Alpini* with ordinary infantry regiments. An Ethiopian assessment of the Italian army was that its officers were very brave, while the ordinary soldiers seemed less enthusiastic, and the traditionally aggressive, locally recruited, *askaris* often took the lead during attacks. On the other hand, a large number of *askaris* deserted because they were so often given the worst jobs. Much of the most serious fighting in the Ethiopian War was at very close range, genuinely hand-to-hand, and it was here that the Ethiopians decided that these new Italian soldiers were 'brave warriors' compared with their grandfathers who had been defeated at the battle of Adwa.

The seven army divisions raised for the Ethiopian War were administratively replaced, back in Italy, with new units whose divisional numbers were 100 higher and had the number II added. Hence the 5th Cosseria Division was replaced by the 105th Cosseria II. Divisions destined for Ethiopia were otherwise named after cities, rivers, mountains or, in the case of cavalry divisions, parts of Italy's ruling dynasty, the House of Savoy. Colonial formations were simply known as the *Divisione Libia* and *Divisione Eritrea*. In reality, however, the new *Divisione Libia* sent to Somalia under Gen. Nasi largely consisted of Eritreans, plus a smaller proportion of Libyans and Yemeni mercenaries recruited from the other side of the Red Sea.

Strategic thinking in the Italian army traditionally owed a great deal to French military doctrine, with an overriding emphasis on the offensive, while defensive operations were seen as a temporary phase prior to a new attack. In East Africa, however, the Italian High Command feared that the Ethiopians would conduct holding operations against Italian forces advancing from Eritrea in the north, while themselves invading Italian Somalia in the south. Consequently, Italian forces on the

Gen. Mehmet Wehib Pasha, leader of the Turkish advisory mission to Ethiopia, at Jijiga in 1936. He is wearing the uniform of a senior officer of the Imperial Guard, though his lambskin *kalpak* is a solely Turkish form of military headgear. It probably dated from his service in the Ottoman army during the First World War.

Northern Front

1st Army Corps: 26th Infantry Division Assietta, 30th Infantry Division Sabauda, 5th Alpine Division Pusteria, 4th Black Shirts Division '3 Gennaio'.

2nd Army Corps: 19th Infantry Division Gavinana, 24th Infantry Division Gran Sasso, 3rd Black Shirts Division '21 Aprile'.

3rd Army Corps: 27th Infantry Division Sila, 1st Black Shirts Division '23 Marzo'.

4th Army Corps: 5th Infantry Division Cosseria, 2nd Black Shirts Division '28 Ottobre', 5th Black Shirts Division '1 Febbrai'.

Eritrean Army Corps: 1st & 2nd Eritrean Divisions plus minor units.

Southern Front

29th Infantry Division Peloritana.
Infantry Division Libia.
6th Black Shirt Division Tevere.
Minor Italian & colonial units.
  Italian forces were also supported
  by the feudal army of the Somali
  Sultan of Olol Dinle

Ethiopian regular troops with an Oerlikon light anti-aircraft gun during the Italian invasion. These weapons were effective and numerous enough to cause Italian pilots problems during several major engagements.

southern front were to act essentially defensively, though this entailed an advance into the Ogaden Desert to forestall any Ethiopian offensive.

The strategy was correct, but the Italians still laboured under some characteristic difficulties. Mussolini had equipped the Italian armed forces primarily as propaganda weapons, a fact brutally exposed in 1940-41. Even after the Ethiopian War had been won, the Fascist government made the invasion sound much easier than it really was in order to promote an image of Italian military power. Another problem which predated the Fascist seizure of power in Rome was a tendency to intrigue among higher general officer ranks, to which Mussolini's persistent interference had been added. Mussolini also downgraded the prestige and authority of the Italian military high command in order to enhance his own status. In reality the success of the invasion of Ethiopia resulted from the Italians achieving huge material superiority, maintained by efficient logistical support to counterbalance the greater individual motivation of Ethiopian troops. The Italians undoubtedly tended to use their relatively few native *askaris* as the 'point of the sword', but Italian *Alpini* also played a major role on the mountainous northern front. In several cases *Alpini* officers were put in command of other forces when operating in particularly steep terrain.

In Ethiopia the Italians' CV 3/33 and CV 3/35 light tanks proved capable of negotiating rough terrain and were effective against limited opposition. On the other hand they were vulnerable even to light anti-tank weapons, and proved tactically less decisive than had been hoped on the mountainous northern front although they did permit greater freedom of movement to Italian columns. Italian light tanks, armoured cars, armed though not armoured trucks, and motorised forces generally had greater impact in the open semi-desert flatlands of the southern front. This was acknowledged both by the Ethiopians' Turkish adviser, Gen. Mehmet Wehib Pasha and by the Belgian mercenary, Lt. Frère. There was, however, no real 'front' in the Ogaden since the Italians operated as columns, foreshadowing the Axis and Allied tactics in North Africa during the Second World War.

The Italians were similarly in the forefront of military ideas in the way they used aircraft as airborne 'cavalry' in this new form of open warfare. Italian planes harassed Ethiopian supply lines with considerable success and helped break the morale of enemy infantry. They also dropped flares to illuminate retreating enemy forces at night. On the other hand aerial bombing became less effective as the Ethiopians learned to spread out and use cover when attacked from the air. In several respects the conquest of Ethiopia, which took seven months and two days, obscured the difficulties faced by Italian forces and gave Mussolini an inflated sense of Italian military power and the effectiveness of his favoured weapon – propaganda.

A Potez 25 two-seater reconnaissance and bomber aircraft of the Ethiopian Air Force. Ethiopian Potez aircraft carried no guns, although they could drop bombs. The Amharic inscription on the fuselage means 'Bird of the Crown Prince'. Other aircraft carried different names, but all of these were removed before the outbreak of the Italian-Ethiopian war. This particular machine (serial number 2) was captured slightly damaged at Akaki airfield at the end of the war, all the others having been destroyed.

GLOSSARY

Italian terms

Alpino soldier in the Italian army's élite Mountain Infantry Corps.

Arditi assault troops in the First World War Italian army and subsequently in the Fascist MVSN.

Askari soldier recruited from the indigenous population of Italian North and East Africa.

Autobilinda armoured car.

Battaglione battalion.

Bersaglieri light infantry sharp-shooters of Italian army.

Brigata brigade.

Bustina side-cap of Italian troops (lit. envelope).

Carabinieri Reali Military Police, senior arm of the Italian army.

Celere motorised forces in Italian army (lit. fast).

Centuria company in the Fascist MVSN.

Centuria Lavoratori Labour Unit in the Fascist MVSN.

Cohort battalion in the Fascist MVSN.

Commando Generale General Headquarters.

Commando Supremo general staff.

Compagnia company.

Divisione division.

Dubat irregular border units in Italian colonial forces (lit. white turbans).

Duce leader, title adopted by Mussolini.

Fanteria infantry.

Granatieri grenadiers.

Gruppo brigade.

Guardia alla Frontiera frontier guard.

Guastatori assault engineers.

Legione regiment in the Fascist MVSN.

Manipolo platoon in the Fascist MVSN.

Milite member of the Fascist MVSN.

Milizia Volontaria per la Sicurezza Nazionale (MVSN) Fascist 'Volunteer Militia for National Security'.

Motomitraglieri machine gunners on motorbikes.

Plotone platoon.

Raggruppamento task force.

Reggimento regiment.

Regia Aeronautica Italian 'Royal Air Force'.

Regio Corpo Truppe Coloniali 'Royal Colonial Troop Corps' of the Italian army.

Regio Esercito 'Royal Army', proper title of the Italian army under the monarchy.

Sahariana tropical service tunic.

Squadra section in the Fascist MVSN.

Takia soft fez headdress of Libyan troops in the Italian army.

Tarbusc tall still fez headdress worn by Eritrean & Somali troops in the Italian army.

Zaptie indigenous Carabinieri or gendarmes in Italian Eritrea.

Zona division in the Fascist MVSN.

Ethiopian, Eritrean and Somali terms

Afanegus Lord Chief Justice.

Agefari Superintendent of Banquets.

Azaz Master of Ceremonies.

Bahr Ghazal Lord of the Sea (traditional title of the ruler of Eritrea before the Italian occupation).

43

Eritrean *askaris* of the Asmara airfield defence unit helping to move a Caproni Ca-101 D-2 bomber of No. 15 Squad., Regia Aeronautica. Airfield defence seems to have been assigned to Eritrean units ever since the first Italian military aircraft, a Farman Type 1914, arrived in Italian East Africa in 1920.

Bajirond Guardian of Royal Property.
Billao traditional Somali dagger.
Bitwoded Chief Counsellor.
Blatta court page.
Blattengueta Chief Administrator of the Palace.
Chitet mobilisation or summons to war.
Degiacc governor of a small province.
Degiasmacc or *Degiacc Negarit* more senior governor.
Dimiphor Ethiopian name for Lee Mitford rifle.
Embilta Ethiopian horn.
Ferenghi white-skinned Europeans (lit. 'Franks', from Arabic).
First Fitaurari Minister of War.
Fute traditional Somali costume consisting of strips of cloth worn across the shoulders and round the body.
Gascegna tribal warrior.
Gebar serf.
Gemgiabiet military warehouses controlled by an imperial officer.
Gibbi nobleman's residence, cluster of buildings rather than a palace.
Kantiba mayor.
Kebur Zabagna Ethiopian Imperial Guard (lit. 'great' Zabanga, from Arabic *kibir*, big).
Lembd Ethiopian cape of animal skin or velvet.
Ligaba Court Chancellor.
Lij prince or young nobleman (lit. son).
Liquemaquas Emperor's double.
Mahel Safari old regular army (lit. army of the centre).
Mekuannen young aristocrat.

Mered Azmatch honorific title given to the crown prince.
Mitraya Ethiopian term for machine gun (from French 'mitraillette').
Nagradas Overseer of the Treasury.
Negarit large Ethiopian war drum used as a mark of rank.
Negus Negast Emperor (lit. Negus of the Neguses).
Negus Ethiopian ruler.
Nevraid ruler of Axum, a semi-religious position.
Ras Ethiopian nobleman or traditional ruler of a province.
Ras be Ras most senior aristocrat (lit. Ras of Rases).
Ras Bitwodded Chancellor.
Scium governor of a district (lit. head).
Selfegna soldier in the regular Ethiopian army.
Shamma Ethiopian male costume, length of cotton which served as a body and head covering.
Shifta Ethiopian bandit.
Shotel Ethiopian curved sabre.
Tripoloc Ethiopian veterans who had served in Italian or British colonial regiments (lit. one who had served in Tripoli in Italian Libya).
Tsehafe Taezaz Minister of the Pen, Keeper of the Seal.
Tukul Ethiopian hut.
Woizero noblewoman.
Zabagna Ethiopian watchman, guard.
Zabanga Gendarmerie for the Addis Ababa area (lit. watchman or guard).

FURTHER READING

Arnold, A.C., 'Italo-Abyssinian Campaign', *Royal United Services Institution Journal* (Feb. 1937), 71-88.

Badoglio, Marshal, *The War in Abyssinia* (London 1937).

Baer, G.W., *The Coming of the Italian-Ethiopian War* (London 1967).

Baldini, M., *Italiani in Africa* (Longanesi 1972).

Barker, A.J., *The Italo-Ethiopian War 1935-36* (London 1968).

Barlozzetti, U., & A. Pirella, *Mezzi dell'Esercito Italiano 1935-1945* (1986).

Bastico, E., *Il ferreo Terzo Corpo in Africa Orientale* (Milan 1937).

Belogi, R., *Regio Esercito Italiano. Uniformi 1933-1940* (Civitanova Marche 1978).

Bianchi, G., *Rivelazioni sul conflitto italo-etiopico* (Milan 1967).

Coffey, T.M., *Lion by the Tail. The Story of the Italian-Ethiopian War* (London 1974).

Con l'esercito Italiano in Africa Orientale (Milan 1936-7).

Crociani, P., & A. Viotti, *Le uniformi dell'A.O.I. (Somalia 1889-1941)* (Rome 1980).

Crociani, P., & A. Viotti, *Le uniformi coloniali libiche 1912-1942* (Rome 1977).

De Bono, Marshal, *Anno XIII: The Conquest of an Empire* (London 1937).

Del Boca, A., *Gli Italiani in Africa Orientale: La Conquista dell'Impero* (Rome 1979).

Del Boca, A., *The Ethiopian War 1935-1941* (Chicago 1969).

Del Valle, P.A., *Roman Eagles over Ethiopia* (Harrisburg 1940).

Emiliani, A., G.F. Ghergo & A. Vigna, *Regia Aeronautica: I Fronti Africani* (Parma 1979).

Gentili, R., *Guerra Aerea sull'Ethiopia* (Florence 1992).

Gentizon, P., *La Conquête de l'Ethiopie* (Paris 1936).

Graziani, R., *Il Fronte Sud* (Milan 1938).

Haile Selassie I., (trans. M. Griaule), *La vérité su la guerre Italo-Ethiopienne* (Paris 1936).

Hamilton, E., *The War in Abyssinia* (London 1936).

Jones, A.H.M., & E. Monro, *A History of Ethiopia* (Oxford 1935).

Julian, H.F., *The Black Eagle* (London 1964).

Konovaloff, T.E., *Con le Armate del Negus* (Bologna 1936).

Lloyd, H.P., 'The Italo-Abyssinian War, the Operations: Massawa-Addis Ababa', *RAF Quarterly*, VIII (1937), 357-67.

Mariotti, D., *In arme sulle Ambe* (Milan 1937).

Matthews, H., *Eyewitness in Abyssinia* (London 1937).

Mockler, A., *Haile Selassie's War* (Oxford 1984).

Montanelli, I., *I Battaglione Eritreo* (Milan 1936).

Mussolini, V., *Voli sulle Ambe* (Florence 1937).

Pankhurst, R., 'The Ethiopian Army of Former Times', *Ethiopia Observer*, VII (1963) 118-43.

Pesenti, G., *La Prima Divisione Eritrea alla battaglie dell'Ascianghi* (Milan 1937).

Polson Newman, E.W., *Italy's Conquest of Abyssinia* (London 1937).

Rosignoli, G., *MVSN 1923-1943 Badges and Uniforms of the Italian Fascist Militia* (Farnham 1980).

Rosignoli, G., *MVSN, Storia, Organizzazione, Uniformi e Distintivi* (Parma 1995).

Schaefer, L.F. (edit), *The Ethiopian Crisis. Touchstone of Appeasement?* (Boston 1961).

Starace, A., *La marcia su Gondar* (Milan 1936).

Stella, G.C., *Album dei gradi, fregi e distintivi del Corpo di Pilozia dell'Africa Italiana (P.A.I.) Africa Orientale* (Ravenna 1989).

Stella, G.C., *Note sui colori delle fasce distintivo delle RR. Truppe Coloniali Italiane e Corpi Armati. Africa Orientale 1885/1941* (Ravenna 1990).

Tomaselli, C., *Con le colonne celeri dal Mareb allo Scioa* (Milan 1936).

Trye, R., *Mussolini's Soldiers* (Shrewsbury).

Vitali, G., *Le guerre Italiane in Africa* (Milan 1936).

Xylander, R., *La conquista dell'Abissinia* (Milan 1937).

Zoli, C., *Etiopia d'Oggi* (Rome 1935).

East African *askaris* of the *Regio Corpo di Truppe Coloniali* guarding a store of abandoned Ethiopian weapons in the closing stages of the Italian-Ethiopian war. It is interesting to note that their European officer has a typical Italian *bustina* side-cap, while the NCO wears the shorts originally reserved for officers in Italian metropolitan units.

THE PLATES

A1: Officer, Kebur Zabagna, Ethiopian Imperial Guard The term *Kebur Zabagna* meant 'Great' or 'Big' *Zabagna,* although it was also used for the officer corps of the Imperial Guard. The guardsmen numbered around 25,000 by 1935, and included many soldiers who had served with the Italian army in Libya or in the British King's African Rifles in Kenya. They were the pride of the Ethiopian army, being equipped with new Mauser rifles and German belts worn over a European-style khaki uniform. Collar patches were red for riflemen, dark green for machine gunners and black for Schneider mountain-gun artillerymen.

A2: Officer, the Mahel Safari, regular Ethiopian Army Officers in the *Mahel Safari*, or regular army, were often dressed in European style. They included men who had studied at the French Military Academy at St Cyr as well as Ethiopian tribal chieftains who sometimes adopted European-style uniforms and even, in the closing weeks of the Italian-Ethiopian War, cadets from the new Ethiopian Military Academy at Oletta. From cork sun-helmets to boots, every element was based upon those of European colonial armies.

A3: Selfegna (ordinary soldier), the Mahel Safari regular Ethiopian Army The *Mahel Safari* under the command of the Emperor Haile Selassie largely consisted of *Selfegna*, ordinary soldiers equipped according to European standards. Their uniforms were, however, locally made, and several times Emperor Haile Selassie felt obliged to issue direct orders to the officers of the *Mahel Safari*, instructing them to ensure that their men's traditional white clothing be dyed something at least approaching khaki. Such soldiers were armed with whatever rifles were available, including modern Mausers, Männlichers, Lebels, Lee-Metfords, Moisins and Italian Männlicher Carcanos, as well as much older Vetterlis, le Gras and Martini-Henry guns.

B1: Embilta player Following centuries-old tradition, the bulk of the Ethiopian army consisted of feudal troops summoned by means of a *Chitet* (muster) or call to arms. Traditional *embiltas* or horns, as well as *negarits* or drums sounded ceaselessly during battles, and even when the army was on the march.

B2: Amharic Gascegna, traditional warrior The term *gascegna* referred to feudal or tribal warriors, in this case from the dominant Amharan people of central Ethiopia. Many were armed with a *shotel*, which was the characteristic Ethiopian curved sabre. A traditional medieval concept of warfare remained virtually unchanged among such people. Their costume consisted of a shamma, or length of cotton which served as a body and head covering, with more modern jodhpur-style trousers which had been added at the insistence of the Emperor Menelik II in the late 19th century.

B3: Galla cavalryman Most Ethiopian cavalry came from the Oromo tribesmen, part of the largely nomadic Galla people, who were sometimes allied to the *Negus* and sometimes fought against him as the Azebo Galla did at the battle of Maych'ew. These men wore the distinctive *lembd* or animal-skin cape which could be of lion, baboon or sheep, or of embroidered velvet. Its richness normally indicated the wearer's power or fame as a warrior. This cavalryman is also armed with an archaic Italian Vetterly Mod. 1870 rifle.

C1: Askari, IX Arab-Somali Battalion, RCTC, Somalia The *Regio Corpo Truppe Coloniali* (RCTC or Royal Colonial Troop Corps) in Somalia operated on the southern front during the Italo-Ethiopian War and consisted of 12 infantry battalions. Their khaki uniforms had been adopted in the late 1920s for marching order, while the *askari's tarbusc* headgear gained a khaki covering at the start of the war. Elements from the normal uniform of Italian metropolitan troops were also included, such as the grey-green cape and the puttees. This *askari* is armed with a Männlicher Carcano Model 91 Cavalleria carbine and an infantry bayonet.

C2: Capo (Sergeant), Banda Dubat, RCTC, Somalia The name *Dubat* came from *dub*, meaning turban, and *at* meaning white – hence 'white turbans'. *Dubats* formed Border Bands which were increased by six groups during the early phases of the war. During the final offensive on the southern front the four bands of Colonel Bechi – founder of the *Dubats* – were then added to these six. The *Dubats'* turbans and also the two *fute* – the strips of cloth worn across the shoulders and around the body as a skirt – were dyed khaki. Rank was indicated by lanyards with tassels around the individual's neck; green for *Capo Comandante* (warrant officer), red for *Capo* (sergeant) and black for *Sotto-Capo* (corporal). Their weapons consisted of a Männlicher Model 95 rifle with corresponding undyed leather ammunition pouches and usually accompanied by a *billao* or Somali dagger.

C3: Bulucbasci (Sergeant), Camel-Mounted Artillery, RCTC, Somalia In addition to the *Bulucbasci's* or sergeant's rank badges, (red on black cloth worn on the sleeves) two metal stars were added above the artillery badge on the man's *tarbusc*. For Italian colonial forces, yellow was the distinguishing colour of Camel-Mounted Artillery, seen here on the *tarbusc* tassel and on the sash. Armament consisted of a Männlicher Carcano Model 91 Cavelleria carbine. The Camel-Mounted Artillery batteries were equipped with 65/17 guns transported in pieces by camels.

D1: Cavalry Askari, 'Penne di Falco' (Hawk Feathers) Squadron, RCTC, Eritrea The picturesque tall *tarbusc* with a long feather thrust into the coloured band was characteristic of the Eritrean Cavalry Corps. During the Italo-Ethiopian War these squadrons operated on the southern front and were equipped with Männlicher Carcano Model 91 Cavalleria carbines or Mauser rifles.

D2: Jusbasci Capo, Zaptie, RCTC, Eritrea The *Zaptie* were the native *carabinieri* gendarmes, or police of Eritrea. Their uniforms were distinguished by a metal badge on the *tarbusc,* a blue tassel, red sash and collar patches. The two silver stars on this man's sleeve rank badges indicate 12 years' service, the badges themselves being those of a *Jusbasci* or warrant officer. He is armed with a Bodeo Model 1889 revolver.

D3: Muntaz (Corporal), XIV Eritrean Battalion, RCTC, Eritrea Machine gunners among the Eritrean *askaris* put their distinctive badges on the *bustina* side-caps which were worn by many Eritrean battalions. The red cloth star on the *Muntaz* corporal's sleeve rank badges indicate two years' service. Many native troops in the RCTC continued to use traditional weapons such as this man's reverse-curved sword. He is otherwise armed with a Männlicher Carcano Model 91 Fanteria rifle.

E1: Infantry Corporal, 60th Calabria Regiment, Sila Division This soldier is typical of the infantryman on colonial service. The popular sand-goggles and a Männlicher Carcano Model 91 Fanteria rifle complete his equipment. The national cockade beneath the goggles is surmounted by a metal corps badge.

E2: Vice Capo Squadra Ardito, MVSN The *bustina* side-cap was very popular among both MVSN Black Shirts and regular army infantrymen. The rank badges of the infantry differed, however, from those adopted by the MVSN. A *Vice Capo Squadra* was equivalent to a *Corporal Major* or senior corporal, and the characteristic *Arditi* ' assault troops' cloth patch has been sewn above the metal divisional badge on this NCO's left sleeve. A plain dagger with a bakelite grip was a characteristic addition to Fascist uniforms. He carries a Männlicher Carcano Model 91 TS (Truppe Speciali, or Special Troops) rifle.

E3: Corporal Major, 3rd Bersaglieri Regiment, Colonna Celere Photographs taken during the *Bersaglieris'* march to Gondar often show uniforms being worn without shirts. The typical helmet plume is made of 105 capon feathers. He has a Männlicher Carcano Model 91 TS (Truppe Speciali) rifle and an unofficial, hand painted stencil badge on his pith helmet.

F1: Primo Capo Squadra (Sergeant Major), MVSN This man is typical of the appearance of the Black Shirts or Fascist *Milizia Volontaria per la Sicurezza Nazionale* (Volunteer Militia for National Security). The rank badge of a *Primo Capo Squadra*, or sergeant major is worn on the left side of his cork helmet. He is armed with a Breda Mod. 30 machine gun and wears Continental grey-green leather tool pouches.

F2: Infantry Tenente (Lieutenant), 63rd Cagliari Regiment, Assietta Division Normal shoulder straps from the metropolitan uniform, as worn in Italy, have been added to this *Tenente's* jacket. The clothing itself is a winter version of the tropical uniform. The regimental collar patches are also surmounted by metal stars, while his weapon is a Beretta Model 1934 pistol.

F3: Milite, 221st 'Italiani all'Estero Legion', 6th Tevere Division, MVSN An MVSN *Legion* was equivalent to a regiment in the regular army. This unit, distinguished by a blue cape and puttees, fought on the southern front. The metal corps badge was applied directly to the cork helmet without a national cockade. Unlike the metal badge of the famous '28 Ottobre' Division, whose name commemorated the Fascist March on Rome in 1922, this '28 Ottobre's' Divisional badge on the left sleeve is made of cloth.

G1: Milite, III Centuria Lavoratori, MVSN Many photographs of Fascist militiamen and ordinary Italian infantry soldiers taken during the Italo-Ethiopian War show them in this guise. In many ways it was the sheer hard work of building new roads such as the one linking the northern front to the Ethiopian capital, Addis Ababa, which won the war for Italy. The *Centuria Lavoratori* or Workers Centuries added a black cloth cockade beneath the distinctive metal badge on their cork helmets. Also note his Continental grey-green woollen breeches and puttees.

G2: Capitano, XLV Eritrean Battalion, RCTC, Eritrea Italian officers of the native *askari* battalions wore their battalion's typical coloured sashes. Their shoulder strap piping also

Italian soldiers on the railway from Djibouti to the Ethiopian capital of Addis Ababa salute their flag. This followed the entry of the Italian army into Dire Dawa on 9 May 1936, an event which effectively marked the end of the war and was felt by Italian troops to have avenged the Italian defeat at Adwa 40 years earlier.

displayed the same battalion colours. A metal corps badge is also fastened to the national cockade on this officer's cork helmet. His pistol is a Beretta Model 1934.

G3: Alpino, 11th Regiment, Pusteria Division: This figure is based on a photograph taken at the end of the bitterly fought battle of Maych'ew. The *Alpino* has his cartridge pouch strap wrapped around his waist. An embroidered black woollen badge and raven feathers are also characteristic of this élite Mountain Infantry Corps. His rifle is a Männlicher Carcano Model 91 Fanteria.

H1: Pilot Capitano, Regia Aeronautica The *sahariana* general purpose bush-jacket became very popular, even within Italy. Though originally worn by officers, its use soon spread among ordinary soldiers and native troops. The shoulder straps of a metropolitan uniform, have been added to the *sahariana*. They indicate both corps and rank insignia. An airman's uniform characteristically included *sahariana*, shorts and boots.

H2: Pilot Capitano, 15th 'La Disperata' Squadron in flying gear The 15th *'La Disperata' Bombardamento Terrestre* Squadron was attached to the 4th Gruppo based at Asmara in Eritrea. It was regarded as the most Fascist unit in the Italian Air Force. The flying suit, helmet, goggles and large pockets for maps were common to almost all airmen in the 1930s, when most military aircraft still had open cockpits. Behind this pilot is a Fiat Revelli Mod. 14 machine gun.

H3: Askari, VIII Libyan Infantry Battalion, Libia Division The three infantry regiments of the *Libia* Division consisted of the II, III, IV, Y, VIII, IX and X Battalions, operating on the southern front. They often wore a special khaki *takia* headdress, or characteristic soft Libyan fez with the Libyan infantry metal badge. The colour of the *askari's* sash indicates his battalion. This soldier's rifle is a Männlicher Carcano Model 91 Fanteria with its distinctive ammunition belt.

47

Notes sur les planches en couleur

A1 Officier du Kebur Zabagna, armée éthiopienne impériale. Ils étaient équipés de fusils Mauser neufs et portaient une ceinture allemande sur un uniforme kaki de style européen. **A2** Officier du Mahel Safari, arme éthiopienne régulière. Des casques coloniaux en liège aux bottes, chaque élément était inspiré de l'uniforme des armées coloniales européennes. **A3** Selfegna, simple soldat de l'armée éthiopienne régulière Mahel Safari. Le *Mahel Safari*, commandé par l'Empereur Haile Selassie, était principalement composé de *Selfegna* armés de divers types de fusils.

B1 Joueur d'Embilta Les *embiltas* (cors) traditionnels ainsi que les *negarits* (tambours) résonnaient continuellement durant les combats, et mîme durant les marches. **B2** Amharic Gascegna, guerrier traditionnel. Beaucoup d'entre eux étaient armés d'un *shotel*, le sabre recourbé typique. Ils portaient un *shamma* ou pièce de coton qui servait de vêtement et de couvre-chef, avec un pantalon plus moderne du genre jodhpur. **B3** Cavalier galla. La plupart des membres de la cavalerie éthiopienne venaient de la tribu Oromo, qui faisait partie du peuple Galla, composé principalement de nomades. Ces hommes portaient une *lembd* (cape en peau) distinctive.

C1 Askari du Ixe bataillon RCTC arabo-somalien, Somalie. Les *Region Corpo Truppe Coloniali* (RCTC ou Troupes Coloniales Royales) portaient des éléments de l'uniforme conventionnel des troupes métropolitaines italiennes, comme la cape et les bandes molletières. Il est armé d'une carabine Männlicher Carcano Modèle 91 et d'une baïonnette d'infanterie. **C2** Capo banda Dubat, Sergent RCTC, Somalie. Le turban des *Dubats* et les deux *fute* ou bandes de tissu portées en travers des épaules et enroulées autour du corps comme une jupe, étaient teints de couleur kaki. Leurs armes étaient un fusil Männlicher Modèle 95, généralement assorti d'un *billao* ou poignard somalien. **C3** Bulucbasci de l'artillerie montée à dos de chameau, Sergent RCTC, Somalie Le jaune était la couleur distinctive de l'artillerie montée à dos de chameau, que l'on retrouve ici sur le pompon *tarbusc* et sur la ceinture. L'arme était une carabine Cavalleria Männlicher Carcano Modèle 91.

D1 Askari de cavalerie du 'Penne di Falco' (Plumes de faucon), RCTC, Eritrée. Le grand *tarbusc*, orné d'une longue plume enfoncée dans la bande colorée, était la caractéristique de la cavalerie d'Eritrée. Ils étaient équipés de carabines Cavalleria Männlicher carcano Modèle 91 ou de fusils Mauser. **D2** Jusbasci Capo, Zaptie, RCTC, Eritrée. Leurs uniformes se différenciaient par un badge métallique sur le *tarbusc*, par un pompon bleu, une ceinture rouge et des écussons de col. Il est armé d'un revolver Bodeo modèle 1889. **D3** Muntaz, XIVe bataillon d'Eritrée, Caporal RCTC, Eritrée. De nombreux soldats africains du RCTC continuèrent d'utiliser des armes traditionnelles, comme cette épée recourbée. Il est également armé d'un fusil Fanteria Männlicher Carcano Modèle 91.

E1 Primo Capo Squadra, Sergent Major MVSN Chemise noire ou fasciste typique de la *Milizia Volontaria per la Sicurezza Nazionale* (Milice volontaire pour la sécurité nationale). Il porte une carabine Cavalleria Männlicher Carcano Modèle 91 avec une cartouchière Modèle 1925. **E2** Tenente d'infanterie, Lieutenant, 63e régiment de Cagliari, Division Assietta. Les épaulettes normales de l'uniforme métropolitain ont été rajoutées à sa veste. Les écussons régimentaires sur son col sont également surmontés par des étoiles métalliques alors que son arme est un pistolet Beretta modèle 1934. **E3** Askari, VIIIe bataillon d'infanterie de Libye, Division Libia. Ils portaient souvent un couvre-chef spécial ou *takia* ou un fez souple libyen typique. La couleur de sa ceinture indique de quel bataillon il provient. Son fusil est un Fanteria Männlicher Carcano Modèle 91 avec sa cartouchière.

F1 Caporal d'Infanterie, 60e régiment de Calabre, Division Sila Soldat d'infanterie typique en service colonial. Les lunettes de protection contre le sable, très populaires, et un fusil Fanteria Männlicher Carcano modèle 91 viennent compléter son matériel. **F2** Vice Capo Squadra Ardito, MVSN. Le béret *bustina* était très apprécié par les Chemises noires MVSN et par les soldats d'infanterie de l'armée régulière. Les badges de grade MVSN étaient différents de ceux de l'infanterie. Un poignard simple avec poignée en bakélite était souvent ajouté à l'uniforme fasciste. **F3** Pilote Capitino, Regia Aeronautica: La veste saharienne *sahariana* devint très populaire. Les épaulettes d'un uniforme métropolitain ont été ajoutées. Elles indiquent le corps et le grade.

G1 Milite, III Centuria Lavoratori, MVSN Les *Centuria Lavoratori* ou centuries des travailleurs ajoutaient une cocarde en étoffe noire sous le badge métallique distinctif sur leur casque en liège. **G2** Capitano, XLVe bataillon d'Eritrée, RCTC, Eritrée. Les officiers italiens des bataillons africains *askari* portaient la ceinture colorée de leur bataillon avec un passepoil assorti sur les épaulettes. Son pistolet est un Beretta Modèle 1934. **G3** Alpino, 11e régiment, Division Pusteria. Il porte sa cartouchière autour de la taille. Son fusil est un Fanteria Männlicher Carcano Modèle 91.

H1 Caporal-chef du 3e régiment Bersaglieri, Colonna Celere. Le panache typique du casque est composé de 105 plumes de chapon. Un badge métallique de corps est fixé sur la cocarde nationale. Il porte une mitraillette Breda Modèle 30. **H2** Capitano Pilote du 15e Escadron 'La Disperata' en uniforme de vol. La combinaison de pilote, le casque, les lunettes et les grandes poches pour les cartes étaient communs à presque tous les aviateurs des années 30. Derrière lui se trouve une mitraillette Fiat Revelli Modèle 14. **H3** Milite, 221e Légion 'Italiani all'Estero', 6e division Tevere, MVSN. Le badge de corps métallique était appliqué directement sur le casque en liège, sans cocarde nationale. Son fusil est un Männlicher Modèle 95.

Die farbtafeln

A1 Offizier der *Kebur Zabagna*, äthiopische kaiserliche Armee. Die Offiziere waren mit neuen Mauser-Gewehren und deutschen Koppeln, die über einer khakifarbenen Uniform im europäischen Stil getragen wurden, ausgestattet. **A2** Offizier in der *Mahel Safari*, reguläre äthiopische Armee. Angefangen bei den Kork-Sonnenhelmen bis zu den Stiefeln waren alle Elemente der Uniform denen der europäischen Kolonialarmeen nachempfunden. **A3** *Selfegna*, gemeiner Soldat der *Mahel Safari*, reguläre äthiopische Armee. Die *Mahel Safari*, deren Befehlshaber der Kaiser Haile Selassie war, bestand zum Grofiteil aus *Selfegna*, die mit den jeweils vorhandenen Gewehren ausgerstetüwaren.

B1 *Embilta*-Spieler. Die traditionellen *Embiltas* oder Hörner sowie *Negarits* oder Trommeln erklangen während der Schlacht unterbrochen und wurden sogar auf dem Marsch gespielt. **B2** Amharischer *Gascegna*, traditioneller Krieger. Viele dieser Männer trugen einen *Shotel* bei sich, den typischen äthiopischen Krummsäbel. Sie waren mit einer *Shamma*, also einem Stück Baumwollstoff, das sowohl den Körper bedeckte, und moderneren jodh-purähnlichen Hosen bekleidet. **B3** Galla-Kavallerist. Der Grofiteil der äthiopischen Kavallerie wurde aus dem Stamm der Oromo, der zu der großteils nomadischen Bevölkerungsgruppe Galla gehörte, rekrutiert. Diese Männer waren mit dem charakteristischen *Lembd* beziehungsweise einem Umhang aus Tierfell bekleidet.

C1 *Askari* des IX. arabisch-somalischen Bataillons RCTC, Somalia. Die *Regio Corpo Truppe Coloniali* (RCTC, Königliches Kolonialtruppenkorps) wies Elemente der normalen Uniform der Truppen des italienischen Mutterlandes auf, so etwa den Umhang und die Wickelgamaschen. Der abgebildete Soldat ist mit einem Kavalleriekarabiner Männlicher-Carcano, Modell 91, und einem Infanteriebajonett bewaffnet. **C2** *Capo Banda Dubat*, Feldwebel RCTC, Somalia. Der Turban der *Dubats* und die beiden *Fute*, beziehungsweise Stoffstreifen, die über die Schulter und um den Krüper geschlungen wurden und eine Art Rock bildeten, waren khakifarben eingefärbt. Die Waffen bestanden aus einem Männlicher-Gewehr, Modell 95, und üblicherweise aus einem *Billao*, also einem somalischen Dolch. **C3** *Bulucbasci* der kamelberittenen Artillerie, Feldwebel RCTC, Somalien. Die Erkennungsfarbe der kamelberittenen Artillerie war gelb, wie hier anhand der *Tarbusc*-Quaste und der Schärpe erkenntlich ist. Die Bewaffnung bestand aus einem Kavalleriekarabiner Männlicher-Carcano, Modell 91.

D1 Kavallerie-*Askari* der 'Penne di Falco' (Falkenfedern), RCTC, Eritrea. Der hohe *Tarbusc*, bei dem eine lange Feder in das farbige Fand gesteckt wurde, war typisch für das eritreische Kavalleriekorps. Die Soldaten waren mit Männlicher-Carcano Kavalleriekarabinern, Modell 91, oder Mauser-Gewehren ausgerüstet. **D2** *Jusbasci Capo*, Zaptie, RCTC, Eritrea. Die Uniformen dieser Soldaten unterschieden sich durch ein Metallabzeichen auf dem *Tarbusc*, eine blaue Quaste, eine rote Schärpe und Kragenspiegel. Der abgebildete Soldat ist mit einem Bodeo-Revolver, Modell 1889, bewaffnet. **D3** *Muntaz*, XIV. eritreisches Bataillon, Obergefreiter RCTC, Eritrea. Viele erkennbare Truppen im RCTC benutzten auch weiterhin herkömmliche Waffen, wie etwa das rückwärtig gebogene Schwert dieses Soldaten. Er ist zusätzlich mit einem Männlicher-Carcano Fanteria-Gewehr, Modell 91, bewaffnet.

E1 *Primo Capo Squadra*, Hauptfeldwebel MVSN. Ein typisches Schwarzhemd, beziehungsweise ein Faschist im Dienst der *Milizia Volontaria per la Sicurezza Nazionale* (Freiwillige Bürgerwehr für nationale Sicherheit). Er hat einen Kavalleriekarabiner Männlicher-Carcano, Modell 91, und Munitionstaschen Modell 1925 bei sich. **E2** Infanterie-*Tenente*, Leutnant, 63. Cagliari-Regiment, Assietta-Division. An der Jacke dieses Soldaten wurden die normalen Schulterklappen der Uniform des Mutterlandes hinzugefügt. Über den Kragenspiegeln des Regiments befinden sich Sterne aus Metall. Bei seiner Waffe handelt es sich um eine Beretta-Pistole, Modell 1934. **E3** *Askari*, VIII. libysches Infanterie-Bataillon, Libyen-Division. Die Soldaten trugen häufig eine spezielle khakifarbene *Takia*-Kopfbedeckung oder den typischen, weichen libyschen Fes. Die Farbe der Schärpe macht das Bataillon erkenntlich. Bei seiner Waffe handelt es sich um eine Männlicher-Carcano Fanteria, Modell 91, mit Munitionsgörtel.

F1 Infanteriegefreiter, 60. Calabria-Regiment, Sila-Division. Die Abbildung zeigt einen typischen Infanteristen im Kolonialdienst. Die beliebte Sandschutzbrille und ein Männlicher-Carcano Fanteria-Gewehr, Modell 91, vervollständigen seine Ausrüstung. **F2** *Vice Capo Squadra Ardito*, MVSN. Die *Bustina*-Seitenmütze war bei den Schwarzhemden der MVSN und den Infanteristen der regulären Armee sehr beliebt. Die Rangabzeichen der MVSN unterschieden sich von denen der Infanterie. Ein einfacher Dolch mit Bakelitgriff war ein charakteristisches Extra bei der Uniform der Faschisten. **F3** *Pilot Capitano, Regia Aeronautica*. Die vielseitige Buschjacke *Sahariana* erfreute sich grofler Beliebtheit. Es wurden die Schulterklappen der Uniform des Mutterlandes hinzugefügt. Sie bezeichnen sowohl die Zugehörigkeit zu einem bestimmten Korps als auch den Rang.

G1 *Milite, III. Centuria Lavoratori*, MVSN. Die *Centuria Lavoratori*, 'Jahrhunderte der Arbeiter', fügte auf dem Korkhelm unterhalb des charakteristischen Metallabzeichens eine schwarze Tuchkokarde hinzu. **G2** *Capitano*, XLV. eritreisches Bataillon, RCTC, Eritrea. Die italienischen Offiziere der einheimischen *Askari*-Bataillone trugen die farbige Schärpe ihres Bataillons und farblich passende Vorstöße an den Schulterklappen. Bei der Pistole handelt es sich um eine Beretta, Modell 1934. **G3** *Alpino*, 11. Regiment, Pusteria-Division. Die Patronentasche wird um die Taille getragen. Bei seinem Gewehr handelt es sich um einen Männlicher-Carcano, 6 Fanteria.

H1 Obergefreiter des 3. Bersaglieri-Regiments, Colonna Celere. Der typische Helmbusch besteht aus 105 Kapaunfedern. Über der Landeskokarde ist ein Korpsabzeichen aus Metall angebracht. Der Soldat hat ein Breda-Maschinengewehr, Modell 30, bei sich. **H2** *Capitano*-Pilot der 15. Schwadron 'La Disperata' in Fliegerausrüstung. Die Flieger in den 30er Jahren hatten fast alle den Fliegeranzug, den Helm, die Fliegerbrille un groflen Kartentaschen gemeinsam. Hinter dem Piloten sieht man ein Fiat-Revelli-Maschinengewehr, Modell 14. **H3** Milite, 221. 'Italiani all'Estero Legion', 6. Tevere-Division, MVSN. Das Korpsabzeichen aus Metall wurde ohne Landeskokarde direkt auf dem Korkhelm angebracht. Bei seinem Gewehr handelt es sich um eine Männlicher